# Project 2025 Explained

A Simplified Version of the 900-Page Report Outlining Key Policies and Their Implications for America

## Ryan W. Wethington

# Table of Contents

# Introduction

Project 2025 is a comprehensive plan to prepare a future conservative administration to govern the United States effectively. Initiated by The Heritage Foundation, this project involves a coalition of over 50 conservative organizations, each contributing their expertise and resources to develop a unified strategy for the next conservative administration. The central idea behind Project 2025 is to ensure that by January 20, 2025, a conservative administration is fully prepared to take office and implement its policy agenda. This preparation includes having detailed policy proposals and assembling a team of trained and vetted personnel ready to assume key government positions.

The project builds on the 1980 Mandate for Leadership legacy, which was instrumental in guiding President Ronald Reagan's administration. Recognizing the increased complexity of the federal government, Project 2025 emphasizes early and thorough preparation to navigate and reform the administrative state effectively.

Key components of Project 2025 include:

- <u>Policy Development</u>: Creating a detailed, agency-by-agency policy agenda that outlines conservative priorities and strategies for governance.

- <u>Personnel Recruitment</u>: Building a database of qualified individuals who align with the conservative agenda and can fill critical roles in the administration.
- <u>Training Programs</u>: Establishing the Presidential Administration Academy to educate incoming officials on government operations and expectations.
- <u>Transition Planning</u>: Developing comprehensive plans for a smooth and effective transition of power, ensuring that the new administration can hit the ground running.

Project 2025: The Conservative Leadership Mandate is a 900-page document detailing the plan for the first 180 days of a conservative presidency. It's more than just a document; it's a comprehensive strategy based on four pillars.

- **Pillar One**: The book serves as the policy guide. Its purpose is to reshape federal policy and shift societal norms in America to align with conservative values.
- **Pillar Two**: The personnel database compiles conservative scholars, academics, and policy experts. This "conservative-only LinkedIn" aims to have at least 20,000 recruits ready to fill positions, streamlining the confirmation process.
- **Pillar Three**: The presidential administration academy is an online training program for potential employees under a conservative president, designed for quick deployment.

- **Pillar Four**: The 180-day playbook outlines transition plans driven by the policy agenda. If the policy agenda is the guidebook, the 180-day playbook is the roadmap.

Project 2025 is more than just a policy guide; it is a call to action for conservatives across the country to join in the effort to restore and strengthen American values and governance. The project's ultimate goal is to create a government that is more accountable, efficient, and aligned with the principles of liberty and justice. By consolidating the efforts of various conservative organizations and experts, Project 2025 aims to provide a clear and actionable blueprint for the next conservative administration, ensuring it is ready to lead from day one and address the nation's challenges.

## Purpose of the Book

The primary purpose of this book is to provide a simplified and comprehensive guide to understanding Project 2025. Given the complexity and depth of the original 900-page report, this condensed version aims to make the key objectives, strategies, and expected impacts accessible to a broader audience. By breaking down the essential elements of Project 2025, this book seeks to inform and engage readers about the future direction of conservative governance in America.

This book is designed for anyone interested in the future of American policy and governance, from policymakers and political enthusiasts to everyday citizens. It aims to demystify the detailed plans and proposals of Project 2025, presenting them in a clear and straightforward manner. By doing so, it hopes to foster a better understanding of the potential changes and improvements that the next conservative administration intends to implement.


Let's get started!

# 1. Background and History

Project 2025 emerges from a long-standing tradition of conservative thought and action aimed at shaping American governance according to liberty, limited government, and individual responsibility principles. To understand the significance of Project 2025, it is essential to explore its historical context, tracing the evolution of conservative policy initiatives and the political landscape that necessitated such an ambitious project.

The roots of modern conservative policy movements can be traced back to the mid-20th century when America faced significant ideological and political shifts. The post-World War II era saw the rise of the Cold War, prompting a need for strong, principled leadership to counter the spread of communism. Conservative intellectuals like William F. Buckley Jr. and Russell Kirk laid the philosophical foundations for a renewed focus on traditional values, free-market economics, and anti-communism.

In 1973, The Heritage Foundation was established as a think tank dedicated to promoting conservative public policies. The organization was founded by Paul Weyrich, Edwin Feulner, and Joseph Coors to provide policymakers with rigorous research and analysis grounded in conservative principles. Heritage quickly became pivotal in shaping conservative thought and policy, advocating for policies emphasizing limited government, free enterprise, and individual liberty.

A critical milestone in conservative policy planning was the "Mandate for Leadership" publication in 1980. As Ronald Reagan prepared to assume the presidency, The Heritage Foundation released this comprehensive policy guide, detailing over 2,000 specific recommendations for reforming the federal government. The Mandate for Leadership was a blueprint for Reagan's administration, influencing significant policy changes in areas such as tax reform, deregulation, and defense.

Ronald Reagan's presidency (1981-1989) marked a transformative period for conservative governance. Guided by the principles outlined in the Mandate for Leadership, Reagan implemented sweeping reforms that revitalized the American economy, strengthened national defense, and promoted individual freedoms. The success of Reagan's policies validated the importance of comprehensive policy planning and the need for a well-prepared transition to conservative governance.

The conservative movement faced new challenges and opportunities in the decades following Reagan's presidency. The rapid expansion of the federal government, increasing regulatory burdens, and the rise of cultural and political progressivism underscored the need for a renewed conservative agenda. The complexities of the modern administrative state and the changing global landscape required a fresh approach to conservative governance.

Recognizing these evolving challenges, The Heritage Foundation launched Project 2025 as a proactive response to the contemporary political environment. The goal was to prepare a future conservative administration to effectively navigate the complexities of the modern federal government and implement a robust policy agenda from day one. Project 2025 builds on the legacy of the Mandate for Leadership, aiming to replicate and expand upon its success in shaping a conservative policy framework.

Project 2025 adopts a comprehensive approach, integrating policy development, personnel recruitment, training, and transition planning. By mobilizing a coalition of over 50 conservative organizations, Project 2025 seeks to unify and amplify conservative efforts, ensuring that the next conservative administration is well-equipped to address the pressing issues facing America. The project emphasizes early preparation, strategic planning, and the importance of a cohesive and coordinated effort.

At its core, Project 2025 envisions a future where American governance is grounded in conservative principles, promoting individual liberty, economic prosperity, and national security. The project aims to restore confidence in government institutions, strengthen the fabric of American society, and uphold the values that have defined the nation's success. Project 2025 aspires to lead America towards a brighter, more prosperous future by providing a clear and actionable blueprint.

## Key Initiators and Stakeholders

Project 2025 is a collaborative effort spearheaded by The Heritage Foundation and supported by a broad coalition of conservative organizations, thought leaders, and policy experts.

### *1. The Heritage Foundation:*

- Role: The Heritage Foundation, a leading conservative think tank, is the principal initiator of Project 2025. Founded in 1973, Heritage has a long history of influencing conservative policy through rigorous research, analysis, and advocacy.

- Leadership: Key figures in The Heritage Foundation, including its executives, researchers, and policy analysts, have played crucial roles in developing and coordinating Project 2025. Notable leaders such as Paul Dans, Director of the 2025 Presidential Transition Project, and Kevin D. Roberts, PhD, President of The Heritage Foundation, have been instrumental in guiding the project's vision and execution.

## **2. Project 2025 Advisory Board:**

- Composition: The advisory board comprises representatives from numerous conservative organizations, each bringing unique expertise and perspectives. This board ensures that Project 2025 reflects various conservative viewpoints and strategies.
- Members: Notable organizations represented on the advisory board include:
    - Alabama Policy Institute
    - Alliance Defending Freedom
    - American Compass
    - America First Legal Foundation
    - Competitive Enterprise Institute
    - Conservative Partnership Institute
    - Family Research Council
    - Texas Public Policy Foundation
    - Young America's Foundation

## **3. Contributors and Authors:**

- Expertise: Project 2025 benefits from the contributions of over 400 scholars, policy experts, and former government officials. These individuals have authored various sections of the comprehensive policy guide, providing detailed recommendations across multiple areas of governance.

Notable Contributors: Key contributors include:

- o Daren Bakst: Deputy Director, Center for Energy and Environment
- o Jonathan Berry: Managing Partner, Boyden Gray & Associates PLLC
- o Lindsey M. Burke: Director, Center for Education Policy
- o David R. Burton: Senior Fellow in Economic Policy
- o Diana Furchtgott-Roth: Director, Center for Energy, Climate, and Environment

## *4. Partner Organizations:*

- Coalition: Project 2025 is supported by over 50 conservative organizations. These partners collaborate to provide resources, expertise, and support, ensuring the project's comprehensive and unified approach.

Key Partners: Significant partner organizations include:

- o American Center for Law and Justice
- o American Legislative Exchange Council
- o Claremont Institute
- o FreedomWorks
- o Hillsdale College

o   Intercollegiate Studies Institute

## *5. Presidential Administration Academy:*

o   <u>Purpose</u>: This academy is a crucial component of Project 2025, designed to train and prepare future government officials. It offers online courses and in-person seminars to educate participants on the functioning of government and the implementation of conservative policies.

o   <u>Leadership</u>: The academy is led by experts from various coalition organizations, ensuring that training is thorough and aligned with Project 2025's goals.

## *6. Personnel Database:*

o   <u>Function</u>: A crucial part of Project 2025 is creating a personnel database, which compiles profiles of qualified individuals who align with the conservative agenda. This database streamlines the appointment process for the next administration.

o   <u>Management</u>: The database is managed by The Heritage Foundation and its partners, who review and recommend candidates to ensure a well-prepared team of officials.

## <u>7. Key Policy Areas and Authors:</u>

- <u>Defense and Security</u>: Contributions by experts such as Christopher Miller (Department of Defense) and Ken Cuccinelli (Department of Homeland Security).

- <u>Domestic Policies</u>: Insights from Lindsey M. Burke (Department of Education), Roger Severino (Department of Health and Human Services), and Jonathan Berry (Department of Labor).

- <u>Economic Policies</u>: Analysis by David R. Burton (Department of Commerce), Stephen Moore (Department of the Treasury), and Karen Kerrigan (Small Business Administration).

- <u>Regulatory Agencies</u>: Guidance from Paul Winfree (Federal Reserve) and Adam Candeub (Federal Communications Commission).

## <u>8. Broad Community Engagement:</u>

- <u>Public Involvement</u>: Project 2025 encourages engagement from conservative citizens, inviting them to participate in the initiative through various channels, including supporting personnel recruitment and policy advocacy.

- <u>Grassroots Support</u>: The project seeks to mobilize grassroots support, emphasizing the importance of public involvement in achieving its objectives.

# The Heritage Foundation's Role

The Heritage Foundation plays a central and pivotal role in the development and execution of Project 2025. As a leading conservative think tank, The Heritage Foundation brings decades of experience in policy research, analysis, and advocacy to the project, ensuring that it is grounded in rigorous scholarship and practical solutions.

## ***Initiation and Leadership:***

- <u>Founding Vision</u>: The Heritage Foundation was founded in 1973 to promote conservative public policies based on the principles of free enterprise, limited government, individual freedom, traditional American values, and a strong national defense. This mission aligns perfectly with the goals of Project 2025, making Heritage a natural leader for this ambitious initiative.

- <u>Leadership Team</u>: Key figures at The Heritage Foundation, including President Kevin D. Roberts, PhD, and Project 2025 Director Paul Dans, have been instrumental in guiding the vision and execution of the project. Their leadership ensures that Project 2025 is strategically aligned with conservative principles and effectively managed.

## ***Policy Development:***

- <u>Research and Analysis</u>: The Heritage Foundation's policy experts conduct in-depth research and analysis across various policy areas. This research forms the backbone of Project 2025, providing detailed, evidence-based recommendations for the next conservative administration.

- <u>Policy Papers and Reports</u>: Heritage produces numerous policy papers, reports, and briefing documents that contribute to the comprehensive policy guide of Project 2025. These documents cover vital areas such as economic policy, national security, healthcare, education, and regulatory reform.

## ***Coalition Building:***

- <u>Collaboration</u>: The Heritage Foundation has leveraged its extensive network of conservative organizations to build a broad coalition for Project 2025. This coalition includes over 50 partner organizations, each contributing expertise and resources to the project.

- <u>Advisory Board</u>: The Heritage Foundation established the Project 2025 Advisory Board, comprising representatives from various conservative organizations. This board ensures that the project reflects various conservative perspectives and strategies.

## ***Personnel Recruitment and Training:***

- <u>Personnel Database</u>: The Heritage Foundation manages a comprehensive personnel database, identifying and vetting qualified individuals who align with the conservative agenda. This database is a critical tool for assembling a capable and committed team for the next administration.

- <u>Presidential Administration Academy</u>: Heritage oversees the Presidential Administration Academy, which provides training and education for future government officials. The academy offers online courses and in-person seminars to prepare participants for the complexities of federal governance.

## ***Transition Planning:***

- <u>Comprehensive Plans</u>: The Heritage Foundation leads the development of detailed transition plans to ensure a smooth and effective transfer of power. These plans cover every aspect of the transition process, from staffing and logistics to policy implementation and communication strategies.

- <u>Historical Precedent</u>: Drawing on the success of the 1980 Mandate for Leadership, which significantly influenced Ronald Reagan's administration, The Heritage Foundation aims to replicate and expand upon this success with Project 2025.

## ***Public Engagement and Advocacy:***

- <u>Outreach</u>: The Heritage Foundation engages with the public through various outreach initiatives, including publications, events, and digital media. These efforts aim to inform and mobilize conservative citizens, encouraging their involvement in Project 2025.

- <u>Advocacy</u>: Heritage advocates for the policies and goals of Project 2025 through its extensive network of supporters and influencers. This advocacy ensures that policymakers and the public hear and consider the project's recommendations.

## ***Continuous Improvement:***

- <u>Feedback and Evaluation</u>: The Heritage Foundation continuously evaluates the progress and impact of Project 2025, seeking feedback from stakeholders and adjusting strategies as needed. This commitment to continuous improvement ensures that the project remains relevant and effective in achieving its goals.

- <u>Adapting to Change</u>: Heritage is prepared to adapt Project 2025 to address emerging challenges and opportunities. By staying responsive to the changing political landscape, The Heritage Foundation ensures that the project remains a dynamic and impactful initiative.

The Heritage Foundation's role in Project 2025 is crucial. From initiating and leading the project to conducting rigorous policy research, building coalitions, recruiting and training personnel, planning the transition, and engaging the public, The Heritage Foundation provides the expertise, resources, and leadership necessary to ensure the success of Project 2025.

# 2. Core Objectives

Project 2025 is designed to prepare the next conservative administration to govern effectively from day one. Its primary goals are to ensure a smooth transition, implement a comprehensive policy agenda, and promote principles of conservative governance across various sectors. These goals center around four main pillars:

- restoring the family,
- dismantling the administrative state,
- defending national sovereignty and
- securing individual liberties.

Below are the primary goals of Project 2025:

### ***Ensure a Smooth and Effective Transition:***

- Plan and organize well before the 2025 inauguration to ensure the new administration is ready to govern immediately.

- Develop detailed transition plans for each federal agency and department, outlining key actions and priorities for the first 100 days.

- Recruit and train a cadre of qualified, vetted, and committed personnel who align with conservative principles and are ready to take on critical administrative roles.

## ***Implement a Comprehensive Conservative Policy Agenda:***

- <u>Policy Development</u>: Create a unified, detailed policy agenda that addresses America's key challenges and promotes conservative solutions.

- <u>Agency-Specific Strategies</u>: Develop tailored strategies for each federal agency, ensuring that all areas of governance reflect the administration's goals and priorities.

- <u>Legislative Action</u>: Work closely with Congress to pass legislation that supports the administration's policy objectives and addresses the needs of the American people.

## ***Restore the Family as the Centerpiece of American Life:***

- <u>Family-Centric Policies</u>: Implement policies that strengthen families, promote marriage, and support parents in their role as primary educators and caregivers.

- <u>Eliminate Marriage Penalties</u>: Remove financial disincentives for marriage in the tax code and federal welfare programs.

- <u>Work Requirements</u>: Reinstate work requirements for welfare programs to encourage self-sufficiency and reduce dependency on government assistance.

## ***Dismantle the Administrative State:***

- <u>Regulatory Reform</u>: Reduce the size and scope of the federal bureaucracy by eliminating unnecessary regulations and agencies.

- <u>Increase Accountability</u>: Implement measures to hold federal agencies and employees accountable for their performance and adherence to conservative principles.

- <u>Streamline Government</u>: Promote efficiency and effectiveness in government operations by consolidating functions and reducing redundancies.

## ***Defend National Sovereignty and Security:***

- <u>Strong Defense</u>: Ensure the United States maintains a robust and capable military to defend against external threats.

- <u>Secure Borders</u>: Implement policies to strengthen border security and enforce immigration laws, protecting American sovereignty and public safety.

- <u>Foreign Policy</u>: Pursue a foreign policy that prioritizes American interests and values, promoting peace and stability through strength.

## ***Secure Individual Liberties and Constitutional Rights:***

- <u>First Amendment Protections</u>: Safeguard freedom of speech, religion, and assembly against encroachments by government and other entities.
- <u>Second Amendment Rights</u>: Protect the right to bear arms and ensure that law-abiding citizens can exercise this constitutional right.
- <u>Privacy and Due Process</u>: Defend citizens' privacy rights and ensure that due process is upheld in all government actions.

## ***Promote Economic Prosperity:***

- <u>Free Market Policies</u>: Implement policies that promote free enterprise, reduce government interference in the economy, and foster innovation and entrepreneurship.
- <u>Tax Reform</u>: Simplify the tax code, lower tax rates, and eliminate loopholes to create a fairer and more efficient tax system.
- <u>Fiscal Responsibility</u>: Reduce government spending, balance the federal budget, and address the national debt to ensure long-term economic stability.

## Advance Education and Opportunity:

- School Choice: Promote policies that expand school choice options for parents and students, ensuring access to quality education regardless of socioeconomic status.

- Higher Education Reform: Implement reforms to higher education that reduce costs, increase accountability, and promote free speech and intellectual diversity on campuses.

- Workforce Development: Invest in workforce development programs that equip Americans with the skills needed to succeed in a changing economy.

## Protect the Environment through Conservative Stewardship:

- Practical Environmentalism: Promote environmental policies that balance conservation with economic growth, emphasizing innovation and private sector solutions.

- Energy Independence: Support policies that enhance American energy independence by developing domestic energy resources and reducing regulatory barriers.

## Foster a Culture of Civic Responsibility and National Unity:

- <u>Civic Education</u>: Promote civic education that instills an understanding of American history, values, and constitutional principles.
- <u>National Service</u>: Encourage voluntary national service programs that foster a sense of civic duty and national unity.
- <u>Community Engagement</u>: Support initiatives that strengthen local communities and encourage citizen involvement in addressing local issues.

## Strategic Milestones and Timelines

To ensure the successful implementation of Project 2025, it is crucial to establish clear strategic milestones and timelines. These milestones provide a roadmap for the administration, enabling it to track progress, make necessary adjustments, and achieve its goals within a specified timeframe. Below are the key strategic milestones and their corresponding timelines for Project 2025:

### *1. Pre-Inauguration Phase (2023-2024)*

<u>Early Planning and Coordination (2023 Q1 - Q2)</u>:

- Formulate the core team and establish project leadership.
- Identify and engage key stakeholders and partner organizations.
- Begin preliminary policy research and development.

## Policy Development and Personnel Recruitment (2023 Q3 - Q4):

- Draft detailed policy proposals for each federal agency and department.
- Create a comprehensive personnel database of qualified candidates for critical positions.
- Initiate the Presidential Administration Academy to begin training future officials.

## Public Engagement and Advocacy (2024 Q1 - Q2):

- Launch public outreach campaigns to inform and mobilize conservative supporters.
- Host events and forums to discuss Project 2025's goals and strategies.
- Begin collaboration with media outlets to promote the project's vision and objectives.

## Finalizing Transition Plans (2024 Q3 - Q4):

- Complete the development of detailed transition plans for each federal agency.
- Conduct final vetting and selection of personnel for key roles.
- Organize transition teams to ensure a smooth handover of responsibilities.

## ***2. Transition Phase (January 2025)***

Inauguration and Immediate Actions (January 20, 2025):

- Swearing-in of the new president and key administration officials.
- Issue executive orders to implement immediate policy changes and set the administration's tone.
- Begin the process of filling critical positions across federal agencies and departments.

First 100 Days (January - April 2025):

- Execute the transition plans for each federal agency, ensuring continuity and stability.
- Prioritize the implementation of high-impact policies and initiatives.
- Launch major legislative efforts in collaboration with Congress.

## ***3. Short-Term Goals (2025)***

First Year Achievements (2025 Q1 - Q4):

- Implement key regulatory reforms and streamline government operations.
- Achieve significant progress on priority policy areas such as tax reform, border security, and healthcare.
- Establish a robust feedback and evaluation mechanism to track progress and make necessary adjustments.

## **4. Medium-Term Goals (2026-2027)**

Building Momentum (2026 Q1 - Q4):

- Continue to advance legislative and policy initiatives per the administration's goals.
- Strengthen alliances with conservative organizations, grassroots movements, and the public.
- Assess the impact of implemented policies and make data-driven adjustments as needed.

Consolidating Gains (2027 Q1 - Q4):

- Evaluate the progress of major policy initiatives and their impact on American society.
- Address any emerging challenges and refine strategies to ensure continued success.
- Expand public outreach and engagement to maintain strong support for the administration's agenda.

## **5. Long-Term Goals (2028-2029)**

Sustaining Success (2028 Q1 - Q4):

- Ensure that the policies and reforms enacted by the administration are deeply embedded within federal agencies.
- Promote leadership development and succession planning to maintain continuity.

- Begin planning for the next election cycle to secure the future of conservative governance.

<u>Legacy and Future Planning (2029 Q1 - Q4):</u>

- Document the achievements and lessons learned from the administration's tenure.
- Prepare for a smooth transition to the next administration, ensuring that Project 2025's principles and goals continue to guide future governance.
- Strengthen the conservative movement by fostering new leaders and expanding the coalition of supportive organizations.

## ***6. Continuous Monitoring and Evaluation***

<u>Ongoing Assessment (2025-2029):</u>

- Regularly review and assess the implementation of policies and initiatives.
- Solicit feedback from stakeholders and the public to ensure alignment with the administration's goals.
- Adapt and refine strategies based on real-time data and changing circumstances.

By following these strategic milestones and timelines, Project 2025 aims to ensure a smooth transition, effective governance, and the successful implementation of a comprehensive conservative policy agenda.

# 3. The Controversy and Implications of Project 2025

Project 2025 is a proposal for how the next president should navigate the administrative state when they take office. It has four pillars: a set of policy proposals for the next administration, a database of personnel who could serve in that administration, a presidential administration academy designed to train that personnel, and a playbook of actions for the first 180 days in office.

Mainstream Democrats refer to Project 2025 as Trump's Project 2025, but it's not something he's put out. While many of the architects of Project 2025 served in the Trump administration, it is not a Trump-approved document or part of his campaign. It's more accurate to say that Project 2025 is a proposal by conservative activists hoping to sell it to Trump if he wins a second term. It's a detailed white paper outlining what strongly right-wing conservative activists and think tanks want a Trump Administration 2.0 to do. Some liberal media and online chatter portray this as sinister, like conservative extremists planning for the next Trump administration. However, the concept of activist groups and organizations coming up with plans for a president is normal—it happens all the time on both the left and right.

Some parts of Project 2025 may be unique but not necessarily sinister. For example, creating a database of personnel for political appointments in a second Trump administration is practical, as they had difficulty filling positions last time. Critics see this as filling the government with Trump loyalists, but political appointees are meant to fulfill the president's agenda. Similarly, a training academy for personnel is not sinister; it's efficient.

The most controversial part of Project 2025 is its policy ideas.

## Climate and Economy

The document proposes slashing federal funds for renewable energy research and investment and stopping the "war on oil and natural gas." Carbon reduction goals would be replaced by efforts to increase energy production and security. This approach has merit. While climate change is real, hamstringing our energy sector won't help. Natural gas, though a polluter, has significantly reduced carbon emissions compared to coal. Climate subsidies for electric vehicles have mostly benefited affluent people and have had little impact on global warming. Americans have struggled to afford gas and energy, which are crucial for the economy. The government should facilitate a more affordable and efficient energy market, potentially including nuclear power development.

Next, the paper presents two competing visions on tariffs: boosting free trade or raising barriers to imports. Project 2025 did not take a clear position on this debate within the GOP.

Economic advisors suggest that a second Trump administration should slash corporate and income taxes, abolish the Federal Reserve, and consider a gold-backed currency. High-income taxes and government spending waste resources; lowering corporate taxes benefits workers by increasing wages and job opportunities and making the economy more competitive. The Federal Reserve has contributed to recent inflation by printing excessive money. While I have concerns about returning to a gold-backed currency, Project 2025's direction has some valid points.

## Abortion and Family Policies

The most controversial part of Project 2025 is abortion and family policies. Project 2025 does not call outright for a nationwide abortion ban. However, it proposes withdrawing the abortion pill mifepristone from the market and using existing but little-enforced laws to stop the drug from being sent through the mail. This issue is complex. While I consider myself pro-life, I tend to support necessary abortion restrictions but not blanket bans without exceptions. Instead of litigating the entire abortion issue here, I want to emphasize that what Project 2025 says about abortion is not what Trump or the Republican Party platform says. The BBC reports that the document differs substantially from the Republican platform, which only mentions abortion once. The platform states abortion laws should be left to individual states and that late-term abortions should be banned. It also protects access to prenatal care, birth control, and in vitro fertilization (IVF). The party platform does not mention cracking down on the distribution of mifepristone.

The party platform is more reasonable and mainstream on abortion than Project 2025. It's unfair for liberals, progressives, and Democratic politicians to take the most extreme ideas about abortion from Project 2025 and claim, "This is what Trump and Republicans will do," when Trump and Republicans have outlined their own platform that says something different. No matter your stance on abortion, don't assign the ideas of Project 2025 to Trump or all Republicans when they have their own, more mainstream positions.

Project 2025 also suggests that the Department of Health and Human Services should "maintain a biblically based, social science-reinforced definition of marriage and family." People interpret this as opposing gay marriage, which seems fair, although it's vague compared to the document's specificity on other issues. Again, there's a difference between Project 2025 and the actual Republican platform, as Trump and his advisers confirmed. That platform specifically removed the anti-gay marriage plank, and Trump is on record supporting gay marriage. So, claiming that Project 2025's anti-gay marriage implications mean Trump will overturn gay marriage doesn't make sense. He has been clear about supporting gay marriage for almost a decade.

According to the BBC, Project 2025 would ban pornography and shut down tech and telecom companies that allow access to it. While porn can be harmful and should be kept away from children, it's a basic question of freedom in a free society. If consenting adults want to create and watch porn, it shouldn't be banned just because others object. In a free society, people should be free to make and view such content.

Banning pornography also presents a huge First Amendment problem. While the First Amendment does not include obscenity, obscenity does not mean all pornography. Some pornographic content has artistic and expressive value. Not all or most porn has artistic value, but drawing that line is difficult, and I don't trust the government to do it.

Banning porn would also create black markets. The porn industry is already problematic, but banning it would make it worse because the demand isn't going anywhere. A black market would arise, and the people involved in porn production would face even worse conditions. While I understand conservatives' concerns about modern pornography, I completely oppose any attempt to ban it.

Trump has never signed on to such a proposal, and I find it hard to imagine he ever would. He has never indicated a desire for a nationwide ban on pornography.

## Education

From Project 2025's education section: the document calls for school choice, parental controls over schools and targets "woke propaganda." Project 2025 proposes to eliminate terms like "sexual orientation," "gender equality," "abortion," and "reproductive rights" from all laws and federal regulations. Many laws touch on these topics, so not using these words doesn't make sense. I understand the desire to make language more factual and less euphemistic, but removing these terms entirely from federal laws is puzzling.

Project 2025 also aims to end DEI (diversity, equity, and inclusion) programs in schools and government departments as part of a broader crackdown on woke ideology. I believe we need equality and non-discrimination, not DEI. Taxpayer dollars should not fund such divisive, identitarian, and often discriminatory programs.

Another controversial point is Project 2025's call to abolish the Department of Education, the federal regulatory agency overseeing education. This might sound extreme, but it's not. The Constitution does not authorize the federal government to have a Department of Education. The current Department of Education has only existed since 1980, so it's not an age-old institution. Abolishing it doesn't mean no regulation or funding for education; about 10% of its duties will be reassigned to other agencies. The most important functions will continue, while the bureaucracy will be reduced. Education regulation will return to the states, allowing them to try different approaches. Successful states will thrive, while others may need to change their ways. This competitive system is a mainstream conservative belief and not as radical as it sounds. Most education funding and provision happens at the state and local level, and the federal department adds unnecessary bureaucracy.

## Immigration

Project 2025's stance on immigration includes increased funding for a wall on the US-Mexico border, one of Trump's signature 2016 proposals. Securing the border is essential to control who enters the country and to stop the flow of dangerous drugs. While building a physical wall is not a new idea, I question its cost-effectiveness, especially since much illegal immigration happens through visa overstays. Building the wall is a long-standing proposal and unsurprising in this document.

Project 2025 also proposes dismantling the Department of Homeland Security and combining it with other immigration enforcement units, creating a larger, more powerful border policing operation. Abolishing the Department of Homeland

Security might sound radical, but it has only existed since 2002. The core functions would be absorbed into other agencies, reducing bureaucracy and bloat. This proposal aims to create a stronger border policing force.

Project 2025's stand on immigration is echoed in Trump's rhetoric and platform to some extent, as is Trump's stance on legal immigration. They want to restrict and decrease the number of people we allow to come here legally. I think that's entirely backwards. We should make it easier for people who want to work, succeed, and contribute to our society to come here. I've never believed that immigrants take people's jobs. Research consistently shows that the economic growth spurred by adding more productive people to our economy creates more jobs than those immigrants take. Immigration only drives down wages for a tiny subset of the American public, typically men without a high school diploma. For everyone else, the effect of immigration on wages is either neutral or positive due to economic growth. Instead of blocking people who want to work and contribute, we should help those without a high school diploma get an education or training to be less vulnerable to competition from unskilled labor. Data consistently shows that legal immigrants commit crimes at lower rates than native-born US citizens.

The issue of illegal immigration is murkier. Project 2025 and the Trump campaign advocate for the largest deportation program in US history, aiming to deport all or most of the millions of illegal immigrants currently living in the US. The scale of rounding up millions of people, many of whom have lived here for years or most of their lives and have families and jobs, would be incredibly disruptive. Instead, we should secure the border to stop the flow of illegal immigration and deport anyone who has committed another crime, especially violent crime or welfare fraud. For the 10-plus million who remain, we need to find a pathway to legal status, not citizenship, but legal status. Many illegal immigrants are hardworking, good people who do not need to be removed from our country. My view on immigration is more moderate and aligns more closely with many Americans. However, on immigration, Trump and Project 2025 are closely aligned, so it's fair to treat them interchangeably on this issue.

## Reclassifying Federal Jobs

Another part of Project 2025 involves reclassifying thousands of jobs in the federal bureaucracy to give the president more power to appoint political appointees instead of career civil servants. According to the BBC, "Project 2025 proposes that the entire federal bureaucracy, including independent agencies such as the Department of Justice, be placed under direct presidential control, a controversial idea known as the unitary executive theory. In practice, that would streamline decision-making, allowing the president to directly implement policies in some areas. The proposals also call for eliminating job protections for thousands of government employees who political appointees could then replace."

The administrative state is out of control. Over 2 million people staff the federal government, but the president only appoints about 4,000, a 1 to 500 ratio. This means we essentially have a fourth branch of government: a vast bureaucracy of civil servants who are entrenched, difficult to fire, well-paid, and wield enormous power over our lives. The regulatory state has grown, and these people's power is astonishing, affecting everything from minor industries to personal rights and liberties.

However, we don't want the entire federal government filled with political appointees, with positions in all departments changing every four years. We need continuity, and not all jobs are political or ideological. However, if Project 2025's proposals aim to give presidents more control over the bureaucracy and, thus, the people more control, I support that directionally.

The problem during the first Trump administration and in a potential future Trump administration is that the average federal bureaucrat tends to be a liberal Democrat, often aligning with the politics of someone like Elizabeth Warren. This vast bureaucracy can impede the implementation of a Republican agenda. When Democrats are elected, bureaucrats are generally ideologically aligned, making governance smoother. This creates a "deep state" that works against Republican interests, making it harder to govern. This situation is undemocratic.

We don't want the entire federal government to be directly politicized, but a 1 to 500 ratio of political appointees to bureaucrats is problematic. Having a government staffed by unelected individuals wielding vast amounts of power is not ideal. Some parts of the federal government, like the Department of Justice, should be more independent and less political, but they have been politicized over the last decade. Concerns about Project 2025's proposals to politicise the federal bureaucracy are valid. However, the notion that lifelong civil servants are not political is false; many are politically biased towards the Democratic direction. This doesn't mean they're bad people or involved in a conspiracy to thwart Trump, but natural biases affect their work. When bureaucrats are overwhelmingly of a certain political inclination, they may not enact the agenda of someone with opposing views with the same enthusiasm or efficiency. Correcting this imbalance is not authoritarian; it addresses an existing problem.

# 4. How Project 2025 Could Affect Low-Income Benefits and Programs

You're not alone if you're worried about how Project 2025 might impact low-income benefits. The "Mandate for Leadership 2025" is 922 pages long and includes many policies. We will discuss the changes recommended for programs like SNAP, TANF, Medicare, and Medicaid. If a policy doesn't directly impact the lives of low-income Americans, it won't be addressed in this section.

## USDA—the US Department of Agriculture

We'll start with the USDA—the US Department of Agriculture, which oversees agriculture, farming, and food benefits like SNAP, WIC, and school meals. Project 2025 recommends simplifying the USDA by moving the Food and Nutrition Service, which manages food programs, to the Department of Health and Human Services. That department already manages other means-tested programs like Medicaid and TANF, consolidating all those programs into one department. Allegedly, this change would streamline the reporting and management of these low-income programs because they would all be handled in the same offices. It would also allow the USDA to refocus on its original purpose: agriculture and farming.

In addition to moving the Food and Nutrition Service, Project 2025 has many other recommendations for SNAP and other nutrition programs. First of all, Project 2025 does not propose fully eliminating SNAP. Despite some claims, the document does not suggest completely killing SNAP. However, it does propose stricter requirements for the program. This is all speculative, and none of this is certain.

First, they recommend reimplementing work requirements. The SNAP program already has work requirements for able-bodied adults between 16 and 59. These rules state that recipients must be working, volunteering, or engaging in work-related activities like employment training to receive benefits. Many states have relied on waivers to avoid implementing these requirements when unemployment is high. The Heritage Foundation wants to make it harder for states to get these waivers, meaning the existing rules would be more strictly enforced.

Next, they want to change the way broad-based categorical eligibility works. This rule makes it easier for someone receiving benefits from one program to qualify for another. For example, you can automatically qualify for Lifeline benefits if you receive SNAP benefits. Some people receive SNAP benefits automatically because they already participate in other programs like TANF, allowing them to bypass asset limit tests. Project 2025 wants to stop this by tightening the definition of "benefit."

Some people have mistakenly concluded that this means you won't be able to get TANF and SNAP simultaneously, but that's not the case. They propose tightening the definition of benefits, making it harder to automatically qualify for SNAP if you get TANF. However, you could still get both if you meet the requirements for both programs.

They also want to re-evaluate the Thrifty Food Plan, a grocery list made by the USDA that shows the cheapest budget to buy healthy food for a family. This list is used to determine SNAP benefits. In October 2021, there was a substantial increase in food benefits due to an update in the Thrifty Food Plan to reflect actual grocery store prices. The Heritage Foundation wants to re-evaluate that change, claiming it's too expensive and that the Thrifty Food Plan was never intended to be updated that way. They believe it should remain cost-neutral and only be adjusted for inflation.

Cost-neutral means the government assumes that the price of everything in the cart changes only by the amount of inflation, not accounting for other price changes. While this doesn't reflect real-world grocery prices, it's how they believe the

Thrifty Food Plan should be calculated, and SNAP benefits are based on this plan. What would happen if the Thrifty Food Plan were re-evaluated from a cost-neutral perspective is unclear. However, if the changes made in October 2021 are undone, it could potentially result in reduced benefits for most SNAP recipients, which is a concern.

Project 2025 also aims to eliminate what is called the "Heat and Eat" loophole. This loophole allows states to increase SNAP benefits if recipients also receive funds from LIHEAP. The Heritage Foundation states that people receiving LIHEAP are eligible for a larger utility deduction, leading to increased food benefits. In the past, some states issued LIHEAP payments as low as a dollar, recently raised to a $20 minimum. The Heritage Foundation wants to close this loophole and standardize the utility deduction, which could result in lower SNAP payments for some users.

To recap, the policy recommendations in Project 2025 could reduce SNAP benefits and make it harder to qualify for them by restricting broad-based categorical eligibility and enforcing stricter work requirements. However, as some have claimed, it would not completely eliminate the SNAP program.

## WIC

The "Mandate for Leadership" book doesn't say much about WIC except for changing how formula contracts are handled. However, it makes many recommendations for handling school meals, specifically targeting the Community Eligibility Provision (CEP). The CEP allows all children in a school or district to get free meals if 40% of the students are eligible for student meal programs. The Heritage Foundation claims that the number of higher-income families receiving free school meals has doubled or tripled since this provision was introduced. Project 2025 asks Congress to eliminate the CEP and stop funding free meals during the summer when children are not attending school. This would make it harder for middle-income families to access school meals during the school year and remove essential support for low-income families during the summertime. However, similar recommendations in the past were not fully adopted, so there is hope this one will also be ignored.

For TANF, Project 2025 recommends increasing work engagement. Currently, TANF requires states to enforce work requirements only for those receiving basic assistance, usually cash benefits, which account for about 22% of TANF dollars. Most TANF recipients benefit from other supportive services like Head Start and childcare. Under Project 2025 recommendations, families would have to meet work requirements if they receive any non-cash benefit worth $50 a month or more for at least six consecutive months.

There is also a recommendation for families who either pay or receive child support. Project 2025 suggests the government require each state to create an easy-to-use app to track child support payments, link bank accounts, and provide one-click payments. Parents should also be able to track informal gifts, such as groceries, clothes, or other contributions, to clearly see how much is being contributed to the child's care.

## Healthcare

Project 2025 also focuses on healthcare. On page 283, they state, "Our deficit problem is a Medicare and Medicaid problem." Therefore, Medicare and Medicaid received numerous recommendations in the "Mandate for Leadership" book.

For Medicare, they recommend reducing regulatory burdens, adjusting pay rate schedules, and making Medicare Advantage the default enrollment option for new beneficiaries. They also want to reform traditional Medicare, which they call "legacy Medicare," to improve price transparency and other aspects.

They propose major reforms for Medicaid, including changing the state waiver process and ending non-healthcare benefits and services. This means ending programs that provide free air conditioners, rental assistance, school supplies, and other non-health benefits through Medicaid. They also want to strengthen asset limits, create "more robust eligibility determinations," and hold states more accountable for improper eligibility determinations. Other recommendations include adding work requirements, time limits, and lifetime caps on benefits, making it harder to get, keep, and use Medicaid in the future.

## HUD, VA, Tax Code, and Social Programs

For the Department of Housing and Urban Development (HUD), Project 2025 aims to reverse HUD's "mission creep." They want to restructure HUD, repeal climate change initiatives, and eliminate the New Housing Supply Fund. They also recommend a rule to prevent non-citizens from living in federally assisted housing, stating that mixed-status families should not live in federal housing. Other recommendations include adding work and work readiness requirements to housing programs and setting maximum term limits for certain residents. They also target "Housing First" policies, which help homeless people secure housing before addressing issues like substance abuse. Instead, they believe mental health and substance abuse issues should be solved first.

For veterans, Project 2025 seeks to expand the VA's Community Care Program and community-based outpatient clinics instead of maintaining "obsolete and unaffordable VA healthcare campuses." They also want to reform the VA disability process to make it faster by increasing automation, hiring more companies to conduct disability exams, and creating a new "Express 30" commitment pilot to resolve a veteran's first fully developed claim within 30 days.

However, Project 2025 is concerned about the VA's schedule for rating disabilities, which assigns percentages to different medical conditions for veterans' disability compensation. They want to revise the list of conditions considered service-connected and update the schedule for new claimants while keeping it fully or partially the same for existing claimants. This could mean new veterans may not be able to claim certain conditions as service-connected, and current veterans could have their disability ratings reduced.

Project 2025 also proposes drastic changes to the tax code, including implementing a two-tier tax system that would eliminate most tax credits and deductions like the Earned Income Tax Credit and the Child Tax Credit. This would simplify tax filing but reduce or eliminate tax refunds, substantially increasing the tax burden on low-income families.

The report also includes recommendations such as eliminating Head Start, closing the Department of Education, and ending student loan forgiveness. Interestingly, the document does not address any recommendations for the Social Security program. The phrase "Social Security" appears only ten times in the entire 922-page document, usually referencing parts of the Social Security Act rather than SSI/SSDI benefits directly. On page 710, the document lists Social Security among "other issues of concern that were not addressed in depth."

Many of these recommendations are not favorable for low-income Americans. If enacted, some of these policies would make life much harder than it already is. However, it's important to remember that this organization has been making similar recommendations for a long time and never gets everything they ask for. The media often highlights the more controversial recommendations to generate clicks, views, and revenue. The reality is that the more controversial recommendations are harder to pass and less likely to be enacted. It's frustrating how some of this is handled, and I know many of you have been worried about things that aren't even included.

I have tried to keep this recap as neutral as possible; however, I hope this has provided you with more clarity and some peace of mind about this document, where it came from, and its potential impact on your benefits. If you're particularly concerned about any of the recommendations, consider contacting your elected officials to express your views. Your voice matters. Remember, these are just proposals, not actual laws.

# 5. Critical Concerns for Veteran Benefits

The world is going absolutely wild over Project 2025. We'll talk specifically about the veteran benefit side in this section.

Two major aspects concern veteran benefits. If you take these at face value, you might exclaim, "This is unbelievable!" First, they propose eliminating the concurrent receipt of retirement pay and disability compensation for veterans. Yikes. Second, they suggest narrowing eligibility for veterans' disability compensation by excluding certain disabilities unrelated to military duties. This one concerns me more than the first. But check this out: the 2017 mandate for leadership recommendation status shows these were adopted by the red side of the aisle.

Republicans are essentially down to implement this. Now, this is 2017. You may ask, "Who was president then?" That was during President Trump's term. If you start Googling this, you'll find a Congressional Budget Office (CBO) report on both proposals. It essentially proposed two things: exclude certain disabilities from veterans' disability compensation and exclude certain disabilities from veteran disability compensation for new applicants.

CBO outlined the potential impacts if these changes were implemented immediately and for new applicants up to 2028. Did this go into effect? The answer is no. This option was supposed to take effect in January 2020, but it didn't happen. The second proposal, eliminating concurrent receipt, was also proposed in 2017 to begin in 2018. This would have eliminated concurrent receipt of retirement pay and disability compensation for military retirees. Did it happen? No, it did not.

Now, let's look at the 2025 updated version. It doesn't specifically address these two issues, but that doesn't mean they won't reoccur. What this indicates is that a party considered taking these benefits away. This is a big deal, especially regarding eliminating veteran benefits or excluding disabilities for new applicants, which would be insane.

Department of Veterans Affairs is in Book 20 of the 2025 mandate for leadership, starting on page 641. The mission statement of the VA is to be veteran-centric. This section implies that the VA under Trump was better than under Biden.

## VBA proposals

Now, let's focus on the VBA side. The main concern is the complexity of benefits, leading to confusion and long-term distrust of the VA. This is a factual statement. Wholesale benefits reform is unnecessary, but managerial approaches and technology tools from the private sector could improve existing VBA activities. This issue is most pronounced in the disability claims process, which needs better management and streamlined procedures.

The VA must improve timeliness in claim adjudication and benefits delivery, aiming for weeks, not months. Project 2025 outlines several changes:

- Identify performance targets for benefits, report publicly each quarter, and use these metrics for consistent improvement. This should not be managed solely by the VA to avoid inflated approval rates.

- Introduce a pilot Express 30 commitment for a veteran's first fully developed disability compensation claim, completing it in 30 days.

- Hire more private companies to perform disability medical examinations. This is concerning due to the current issues with C&P exams. Accountability and transparency are crucial.

- Increase automation and technology use to improve claims processing speed and accuracy.

- Reduce improper payments and fraud, which currently result in about $500 million in annual improper payments.

The VA Schedule for Rating Disabilities (VSRD) has assigned ratings to many health conditions, some unrelated to military service. Further growth in presumptive service-connected conditions has led to increased mandatory VBA spending. The VA plans to reassess the rating schedule, but the process is slow and politically charged.

The proposed reforms do not emphasize a veteran-centric approach. They focus on cost savings and efficiency rather than the needs of veterans. Revising disability rating awards for future claimants while preserving them for existing claimants is essentially taking away benefits. The VBA's budget and personnel strategies suggest more privatization. This genuine concern needs more attention and scrutiny to prioritise veterans' needs.

## VHA proposals

The Heritage Foundation, which is behind Project 2025, does not control the government but serves as an advisory tool. Administrations can adopt or disregard these recommendations.

One needed reform is to rescind all department clinical policy directives that contradict conservative governance principles, starting with abortion services and gender reassignment surgery. The argument is that these do not align with service-connected conditions and follow a leftist agenda. While this is a touchy subject, the argument presented is that these services do not align with service-connected conditions.

Another recommendation focuses on shifting veteran demographics. This may upset older generations as it states that Vietnam veterans are dying and Gulf War/Post-9/11 veterans are increasing. The VA will see a demographic shift from Vietnam-era veterans to post-9/11 veterans.

Community care is central to VHA proposals. The main point of Project 2025 for VHA benefits is the Mission Act, which covers community care eligibility and standards. Community care allows veterans to seek private healthcare covered by the VA in a timely manner. The implication is that the current administration is not adhering to the Mission Act and is restricting veterans' access to community care.

Section 121, developing and administering an education program that teaches veterans about the healthcare options available from the Department of Veterans Affairs. I like this. I don't even know why they're not doing that now. You might question, "What are they doing?" The answer is nothing.

Requiring the VHA to report publicly on aspects of its operation: The VA as a whole, not just the VHA but also the VBA, needs to be more transparent. On the VBA side, why does it take a FOIA request to see the adjudication process for your claim? Report publicly on quality, safety, patient experience, timeliness, and cost-effectiveness using standards similar to Medicare.

Encourage VA medical centers to seek out relevant academic and private sector input into their communities. Conduct an independent audit of the VA similar to the DoD. This might be controversial, but it's necessary. Assess the misalignment of VHA facilities and rising infrastructure costs. Medical facilities that are an average of 60 years old, underutilized, and inadequately staffed in certain urban and rural areas face significant declines in the veteran population and competition for new medical staff.

Embrace the expansion of community-based outpatient clinics (CBOCs) and explore the potential for facility-sharing partnerships between VA and Health Care Systems. A recurring theme here is more privatized care on both the personnel and budget sides.

Extend the term for the Under Secretary of Health to five years: Establish an SES position of VHA Chief Information Officer. Identify workflow processes to bring wait times in compliance with the VA Mission Act. Essentially, make VHA faster. Assess the daily clinical appointment load for physicians and clinical staff. VHA facilities are required to increase the number of patients seen daily to match DoD facilities, with approximately 19 patients per day. Currently, VA facilities may see as few as six veterans per provider per day.

Consider a pilot program to extend weekday appointment hours and offer Saturday appointment options. This is for veterans who can't take time off, lack PTO, or have to drive long distances. Identify clinical services that are consistently in high demand. Assess medical facilities where community care is readily available. Further exploration of leveraging telehealth to reduce personnel costs, especially for remote and rural areas, would benefit mental health services. Assess recruitment and retention in highly competitive medical markets.

Consider aggressively recruiting retired physicians who desire to serve veterans, though this may be challenging. Expand VA tuition assistance in exchange for reciprocal service in rural and understaffed VAs. Examine the surpluses or deficits in mental health professionals. Conduct high-quality assessment EHR initiatives. Basically, the goal is to make it more private. There are a few questionable points, but they are nothing too alarming compared to the VBA side.

## The Bad Side When It Comes to Veteran Benefits

I want to highlight this: "The VSRD"—the VA Schedule of Rating Disabilities, 38 CFR—" has assigned disability ratings to a growing number of health conditions over time." Then it says, "Some are tenuously related or wholly unrelated"—meaning barely connected—to service.

What bothers me is the next statement. It talks about the further growth in presumptive service-connected medical conditions. This refers to the PACT Act, pursued by Congress and VSOs, including conditions like Agent Orange exposure and burn pits. It states, "Increases in mandatory VBA spending in recent years." This indicates that someone influential is saying, "The VA is spending too much on conditions that are barely service-connected." There are many issues, but this one stands out.

We shouldn't take anything too lightly because that's how significant changes happen incrementally. We need to take these things seriously to form logical and thoughtful opinions and express them to our elected leaders. Even though it is a conservative blueprint, Project 2025 is a suggestion for elected officials to pick and choose from. Your elected officials need to know where you stand on VA issues. Silent voices don't get heard, and you might end up with policies you don't want.

This is similar to the Congressional Budget Office complaining about VA spending and suggesting ways to cut costs. There's a lot of money spent on veterans, and sometimes conditions that might not have been directly caused by military service are covered because they manifested during service.

Project 2025 seems to suggest reconsidering the coverage of not directly service-related conditions. This could eliminate conditions that manifest during service without direct cause. For example, if you were exposed to jet fuel and have migraines, there might be a correlation. But if you were doing desk work, maybe not. This could also affect secondary conditions, freeing up money for the VA.

Am I a fan of this? No, I think it's a horrible idea. Even though it might not go to such extremes, it's important to talk about it for awareness. If this were to happen, most likely, current conditions would be grandfathered in, but future applicants would be affected, which is unfair to current servicemen and women.

Recently, the Biden Administration, including the VA, pushed for the one-millionth PACT Act claim, and now there's language suggesting changes to presumptive connections. This could make it harder for conditions like rhinitis, sinusitis, and asthma to be service-connected.

We see one side pushing the PACT Act and the other pushing back against it. This is political animosity, and I don't support it. Veterans should be concerned about recommendations from influential groups like the Heritage Foundation. You should ask your representatives if they support the VBA recommendations from Project 2025. While this might not change anything, it's important to be aware. This concern over VA spending and PACT Act claims is one of the biggest issue I see in Project 2025.

# 6. The Omission of Social Security in the 900-Page Proposal

Do they talk about Social Security in this 900-page proposal? The short answer is no, they don't. After reviewing the 900 pages, I found nothing about Social Security. However, we know the Heritage Foundation created Project 2025, and we know their stance on Social Security.

"To meet our defense needs, Congress has to work to grow our economy and significantly reduce our overall spending. I promise you that come 2025, spending reform will be a top priority for our new Republican majority. These conversations won't be easy, but they are essential for long-term survival. Congress must prioritize the truly essential needs of our nation, with national security at the top of that list."

But where does Social Security fall? Social Security is a vital, essential program. Where does it fall in their hierarchy? Lawmakers like Speaker Johnson don't think we should be spending as much on Social Security. They want to make cuts to Social Security and its administration, which is where

Project 2025 comes in. They might not talk about reforming Social Security, but they do talk about cutting various agencies and replacing staff with partisan employees who support Trump. This would be disastrous because experienced workers in agencies like the Social Security Administration would be replaced by unskilled supporters, leading to a huge learning curve and inefficiency.

Additionally, think about the people currently working in the federal system; many would lose their jobs, which would negatively impact the economy. Even if replaced, the initial job losses would cause financial instability for many.

Regarding Project 2025 and Social Security, the 900 pages don't mention Social Security specifically or its reform. But the Heritage Foundation has made its stance clear. They propose raising the full retirement age to correspond with life expectancy, potentially to 69 or 70, effectively cutting benefits. They also want to means test Social Security benefits, reducing benefits for middle and upper-middle-class recipients. This would significantly impact retirees who depend on Social Security for a portion of their income, forcing them to rely more on other retirement funds, potentially outliving their savings.

The Heritage Foundation also wants to adjust the cost of living adjustment (COLA) to reflect older people better, possibly switching from the CPI-W (Consumer Price Index for Wage

Earners and Clerical Workers) to the CPI-E (Consumer Price Index for the Elderly). This could increase benefits over time but also deplete the trust fund faster. Switching to CPI-E would be more appropriate, but the Heritage Foundation hasn't specified its COLA calculation method. Their goal might be to reduce COLAs to save money, which would hurt recipients by providing less annual adjustment.

It's noteworthy that Project 2025 doesn't include Social Security reform despite covering many other government reforms. This omission is significant because, in 10-11 years, we face a potential 23% cut in Social Security benefits due to trust fund depletion. Interestingly, a 900-plus page plan doesn't address Social Security at all.

# 7. Project 2025's Possible Implications for Medicare

There are four primary goals and principles that Project 2025 aims to change for Medicare:

- **Increase Medicare beneficiaries' control over their healthcare**: Patients are best positioned to determine the value of healthcare services in collaboration with their healthcare providers. They also benefit from increased choices in hospitals, doctors, and insurance plans.

- **Access to reliable information**: Keeping your original Medicare and getting a Medicare supplement is important to avoid losing your original Medicare rights. Unlike Medicare Advantage plans with restrictive doctor networks and prior authorizations, original Medicare does not require such approvals.

- **Reduce regulatory burdens on doctors**: Reducing regulatory burdens allows doctors to focus more on patient care rather than administrative tasks. This aligns with the goals of Project 2025.

- **Ensure sustainability and value for beneficiaries and taxpayers**: Medicare spending on Medicare Advantage was $321 higher per person in 2019 than traditional Medicare. Private insurance companies in Medicare Advantage spent $87 on benefits for every $100 from taxpayers, with significant amounts going to profits and overhead. Reducing waste, fraud, and abuse is crucial for sustainability. However, the use of artificial intelligence to deny claims, as some suggest, is controversial. Recently, CMS prohibited using AI to deny claims in Medicare Advantage plans.

While Project 2025 seeks to reduce waste, fraud, and abuse, it also aims to enhance patient control, provide reliable information, and alleviate doctors' regulatory burdens. However, some proposed measures, like using artificial intelligence for claim decisions, have raised concerns.

Project 2025 recommends making Medicare Advantage the default enrollment option. This would give beneficiaries direct control of how they spend Medicare dollars, but it seems contradictory to remove policies that micromanage Medicare Advantage plans.

In my view, Project 2025 aims to automatically enroll people turning 65 into Medicare Advantage plans run by private insurance companies. Recently, it was revealed that these insurance companies stole $50 billion through misdiagnoses and upcoding. In many cases, providers were unaware of these diagnoses. Some doctors were complicit, receiving bonuses and incentives.

Making Medicare Advantage the default option would save money on commercials, as people would be automatically enrolled in a private managed care program. However, you must pass medical underwriting if you're on a Medicare Advantage plan for over 12 months and want to switch back to the original Medicare with a supplement. This could leave someone with serious health issues, like cancer or COPD, stuck in a Medicare Advantage plan with high out-of-pocket costs. This doesn't benefit taxpayers; it's corporate socialism. Taxpayer money would go to the government, which then disperses it to large insurance companies, subsidizing their profits. Removing burdensome policies that micromanage Medicare Advantage plans might benefit insurance companies, but billions of taxpayer dollars could be siphoned off into profits without oversight.

Project 2025 also proposes replacing the fee-for-service system with value-based payments, claiming it would empower patients. However, this would likely empower insurance company CEOs more than patients.

They suggest removing restrictions on physician-owned hospitals, which currently participate in Medicare just like regular hospitals. This could improve consumer choice and reduce special interests' influence.

Encouraging direct competition between Medicare Advantage and private plans is another proposal. Medicare Advantage offers a wide range of competitive health choices and benefits at a reasonable cost, often performing well in delivering high-quality care.

The biggest burden on doctors is pre-authorizations. When a patient needs an MRI, the doctor prescribes it, but the insurance company often overrides this decision, suggesting physical therapy or weight loss instead. Medicare Advantage is 22% more costly than original Medicare. Prior authorizations are almost non-existent in original Medicare. For instance, a motor scooter or chiropractic procedure might be denied, but these are rare exceptions.

With Medicare Advantage plans, you lose control. Project 2025 wants to make Medicare Advantage the default option, bypassing original Medicare. In 2021, more than 35 million prior authorization requests were submitted to Medicare Advantage insurers, with over 2 million denials. Only 11% of these denials were appealed, and 82% of appeals resulted in overturning the initial denial. This suggests a strategy of denying claims, hoping patients will not appeal.

If you're enrolled with Anthem in 2021 and needed an MRI or surgery, you had to appeal 2.9 times a year on average. This shows how prior authorizations in Medicare Advantage can burden doctors and patients.

Unlike original Medicare, where you can see any doctor without pre-authorization for necessary procedures, Medicare Advantage often requires pre-approval. Original Medicare pays for medically necessary services without pre-approval, and a Medicare supplement covers any remaining costs.

Pre-authorization, pre-certification, or pre-approval is a cost-control process requiring advanced approval from a health plan before a service qualifies for payment coverage.

A New York Times article reported that federal investigators found troubling evidence that Medicare Advantage plans delay or prevent necessary care. Denials for authorizations and reimbursements are common, especially for expensive treatments like skilled care after a stroke. This process causes significant harm, with some patients dying due to delays.

Medicare Advantage denied 13% of pre-authorization requests that would have been covered under original Medicare. Additionally, 18% of payments were denied despite meeting Medicare coverage rules. In 2019, Medicare estimated 1.5 million payments were denied by Medicare Advantage plans, sometimes ignoring completed pre-authorizations and documentation to avoid payment. These denials may delay or prevent patients from receiving necessary care under Medicare Advantage.

The Office of Inspector General study, "Advantage Plan Organization Denials of Prior Authorization Requests Raised Concerns," found that 13% of prior authorization denials were for services that met Medicare coverage rules, likely preventing or delaying medically necessary care for Medicare Advantage beneficiaries. This leads to significant harm and frustration, with some patients even giving up on seeking care. Medicare Advantage organizations denied requests for medically necessary services by applying their own clinical criteria, which go beyond Medicare's rules. This major issue is set to change on January 1, 2024.

The study highlights issues with MRI denials, ambulatory devices, and prior authorization requests for medically necessary services being denied due to unnecessary documentation requirements. Eighteen percent of payment denials were for claims that met Medicare coverage rules. These delays impact service delivery and payment to providers, creating a backlog. Commonly denied services include imaging and post-acute care for stroke patients, as well as expensive Part B injectables.

Under original Medicare, with a supplement, these services are covered without pre-authorization. However, Medicare Advantage plans require pre-authorization, often leading to high out-of-pocket costs and denials. Project 2025 aims to make Medicare Advantage the default enrollment option, supposedly giving beneficiaries more control over their Medicare dollars. However, this is questionable given the burden of pre-authorizations. Another proposal is to reform Medicare Part D and remove the Inflation Reduction Act, which is complicated by a recent Supreme Court ruling that affects federal agency power.

The Supreme Court recently overruled the Chevron Doctrine, shifting the interpretation of ambiguous laws from federal agencies to courts. This could significantly impact healthcare and environmental regulations, allowing companies to seek favorable judicial rulings.

For those on expensive drugs like Eliquis, Xarelto, Ozempic, and Mounjaro, starting next year, after spending $2,000 out of pocket, you won't have to pay for the rest of the year. However, the recent Supreme Court ruling could bring changes.

In conclusion, the impact of these policy changes and court rulings on Medicare Advantage and healthcare costs is significant and should be monitored closely.

# 8. Tax Proposals

The tax section of Project 2025 contains some remarkable proposals that could drastically change the tax system. For example, the section on the Department of Treasury (essentially the IRS) proposes intermediate tax reform. Specifically, it suggests that the IRS should work with Congress to simplify the tax code. One proposal is to create just two tax rates: 15% for most taxpayers and 30% for the wealthy. This would also involve eliminating most deductions, credits, and exclusions. Critics argue that removing legitimate deductions is essentially a stealth tax increase.

Under this proposal, the 15% tax rate would apply to income up to the Social Security wage base (approximately $170,000). Income above this threshold would be taxed at 30%. Additionally, a flat 18% tax rate is proposed for large corporations.

A significant aspect of the proposal is the introduction of a low flat tax rate of 15% for capital gains and qualified dividends, indexed for inflation. This could positively impact the stock market and retirement plans. The proposal also includes immediate expensing for capital expenditures, encouraging businesses to reinvest.

The Project also addresses Democratic policies, criticizing their tax policies and fiscal management. It includes proposals to improve financial regulation, tackle geopolitical threats, and reverse Biden administration policies on equity and climate-related financial risks.

One interesting proposal is the creation of Universal Savings Accounts (USAs), allowing Americans to contribute up to $155,000 a year, similar to a Roth IRA but with higher limits. This aims to improve national savings rates.

Regarding the IRS, the Project advocates restructuring, increasing manpower, and enhancing information technology.

In summary, Project 2025's tax policy proposals seek to simplify the tax code, establish flat tax rates, and encourage savings and investment. The plan aims to overturn recent Democratic policies, claiming they have harmed the economy. While these proposals are ambitious and controversial, they offer a vision for significant tax reform.

# 9. Immigration Proposals

President Biden has made it clear that he is willing to move forward with progressive immigration plans and laws to help immigrants contribute to the United States. He has done this by announcing two new policies set to go into effect around August-September of this year. Spouses and children of U.S. citizens can now get what's called parole in place, special permission to live and work in the United States. This is significant because it allows them to apply for adjustment of status, meaning they can now adjust their status here, even if they crossed the border without permission. Remember that you still have to show that you have resided in the United States for the past 10 years. This does not cover those who have been in the U.S. for less than ten years. However, for those who have been here for ten years or more, regardless of how they entered the U.S., now is the opportunity to get that parole. Once you get that parole, it's your ticket to the green card because it allows you to apply for it while staying in the U.S.

For college graduates, the same thing applies. Once you have an employer, even if you're out of status, you can get a waiver plan through the Department of Labor. This makes it easier for college graduates to get a waiver for overstaying a student visa even if they don't have papers. This special waiver allows you to get a visa, get approved for the waiver, and come back to work for the employer who petitions for you. This is crucial for those who did everything right but overstayed due to unforeseen circumstances.

People often say, "Why, I came the legal way; it's not fair that people came the illegal way." Project 2025 shows very little difference in how they treat legal immigrants versus illegal immigrants. It's in all of our best interests; there's no difference here.

Here are the changes. They are going to replace the USCIS, where we apply for green cards, citizenship, and different types of applications to get status, with one agency focused on the border, called the Border and Immigration Agency. The number one priority of this agency is to implement mass deportations. The goal is to deport 11 million undocumented immigrants, and Trump has stated he will use the National Guard and the military, if necessary, to get as many hands on board, not just immigration agents, but the military and the National Guard to round up millions of immigrants. This will be the biggest mass deportation project in U.S. history.

They plan to achieve this by expanding expedited removal, currently limited to within 100 miles of the border, and to new arrivals who crossed the border illegally within the last two weeks, to the entire country. No place will be safe from mass deportations. Currently, there is a priority list for deportation, but the vast majority of immigrants are not on it. This will change. The agency will not be able to grant forms of relief like prosecutorial discretion and deferred action. They will also revoke protections like TPS and DACA.

However, Biden has announced the redesignation of TPS for Haitian immigrants, meaning even recent immigrants can get TPS to live and work here. They can get TPS if they can show they have been here up to a certain date. This is a piece of good news amidst the potential changes. Well, this will take that off the table completely. There is a big difference between this and what Biden is doing now. Biden is trying to balance immigration enforcement at the border while being fair to immigrants who are already here and contributing. TPS and DACA will no longer be available.

It also calls on immigrants, as it is usually within the Department of Homeland Security's discretion to detain them. They can release them as well. That will be no more. They are saying that all immigrants who they see fit to be detained will be detained. There will be no more releases pending immigration court or other matters. They will be detained, and their cases will be expedited, and they will be removed before they can even ask for any relief as asylum seekers.

Many are angry at Biden because he has implemented something similar now due to the situation at the border, which is dangerous for asylum seekers. Imagine fleeing for your life, thinking you will be safe in America, only to face a higher legal standard at the border. An immigrant might need an attorney ready to argue their case and have a brief ready to show the immigration officer that they meet that higher standard. This goes against the basic American ideal of safety for those fleeing danger.

If you put yourself in the shoes of someone running for their life, the last thing they're thinking about is getting a lawyer at the border and putting a legal brief together to prove their asylum case. That's why there is a process allowing them time to present their case and get representation. Biden has implemented a policy to shut down the border when more than 1,600 immigrants come across, making the situation worse.

Remember the "Remain in Mexico" policy and family separation under Trump? These were egregious actions, taking small children away from their parents at the border. They are still trying to fix this situation. If Trump returns, family separation and the Muslim ban will likely return. Officers will prioritize fraud detection over processing times, causing unnecessary delays and denials. Immigrants and their lawyers will face more harassment based on fraud detection.

They plan to get rid of officers who show any resistance to this agenda and specially train individuals aligned with the conservative agenda. This may lead to biased and unfair treatment of immigrants.

They also suggest eliminating work categories like H2B and H2A. H2A workers are in the agricultural sector, and H2B workers are seasonal workers in industries like hospitality and entertainment. Terminating these programs will cause shortages in these sectors.

For the "haves" and "have-nots," they propose cutting certain visa categories but allowing those who can pay high fees to get in or speed up processing times. Trump has also suggested requiring a bond or deposit of thousands of dollars for visas.

It's important to understand what Project 2025 is about because it affects all of us, not just immigrants. The president can implement these plans through executive orders if Congress doesn't have a conservative majority. We've seen this happen before, and it can happen again. Please ensure you know what's going on and what's at stake.

# 10. Overhauling the U.S. Military to End "Woke" Policies

Project 2025 is a collection of conservative and right-wing policy proposals from the Heritage Foundation to reshape the United States federal government and consolidate executive power should the Republican nominee win the 2024 presidential election. It proposes reclassifying tens of thousands of federal civil service workers as political appointees to replace them with loyalists more willing to enable the next Republican president's policies.

Project 2025 aims to take partisan control of the Department of Justice, the FBI, the Department of Commerce, the Federal Communications Commission, and the Federal Trade Commission; dismantle the Department of Homeland Security; and sharply reduce environmental and climate change regulations to favor fossil fuel production. It recommends abolishing the Department of Education, transferring its programs to other agencies, or terminating them. Funding for climate research would be cut, while the National Institutes of Health would be reformed according to conservative principles. The project seeks to cut funding for Medicare and Medicaid, which concerns those dependent on these programs. It urges the government to explicitly reject abortion as healthcare, stating that life begins at conception, and seeks to eliminate coverage of emergency contraception under the Affordable Care Act, also known as Obamacare. It also proposes enforcing the Comstock Act to prosecute those who send and receive contraceptives and abortion pills nationwide.

Project 2025 proposes criminalizing pornography, removing legal protections against discrimination based on sexual orientation and gender identity, and terminating diversity, equity, and inclusion (DEI) programs and affirmative action by having the DOJ prosecute anti-white racism. It recommends the arrest, detention, and deportation of undocumented immigrants living in the US by using the military to capture them and place them in internment camps. It also proposes deploying the military for domestic law enforcement.

In April 2023, Project 2025 director Paul Dans said it is systematically preparing to march into office and bring a new army of aligned, trained, and essentially weaponized conservatives ready to do battle against the Deep State. More recently, in July 2024, Heritage Foundation president Kevin Roberts said, "We are in the process of the second American Revolution, which will remain bloodless if the left allows it to be." Of interest is that while the Trump campaign initially said the project aligned well with their proposals, it has increasingly caused friction with that campaign. Recently, Trump denied knowledge of the project and disavowed it, even though many of his advisers and former officials of his presidential administration drafted and endorsed it. This document could potentially inform the posture of the Pentagon in the next administration. Although his campaign has distanced itself from Project 2025, it is logical to imagine that the tenets in Chapter 4 could inform the Pentagon's priorities if they take office.

The Heritage Foundation did something similar in 1980, creating a 1,100-page document called "The Mandate for Leadership" that many believe was the blueprint for Ronald Reagan's administration. Heritage wants to do this again with the next administration, which seems broadly aligned with its viewpoints. Heritage is a think tank with corporate positions, and preparing for administrations is not an unusual effort.

## Defense Proposals

Chapter 4, the defense portion of this document, is a mixed bag. It is not controversial if you think about American politics and how we have divided things up. Christopher, a fairly low-level political appointee at the beginning of the last administration in 2017, survived people getting thrown off the island throughout that administration to rise to the level of acting Secretary of Defense, where he sat on January 6th during the insurrection. He has put together a relatively straightforward statement of defense policy that anyone familiar with the Department of Defense from 2017 to 2021 should not be surprised by. This is a restatement of most of the same priorities that were important to the Department of Defense during that administration. China is in the crosshairs as the primary focus of this document. It is pro-technology but doesn't worship technology, which is a difference between this crowd and the current administration, which seems more technology-focused. Christopher Miller and the Project 2025 team are less enamored with technology and more focused on additional resources. They want more money for defense and are vocal about it. They believe the military has to get bigger and is currently strained. So, to a center-of-mass right-wing conservative like I am, there's a lot in this document to like. There's also a lot to be wary of. I don't like the China focus because our Department of Defense must be big enough to represent our global focus and responsibilities.

This document has a good deal about the people of the force, how they are led, the degree to which they are politicized, and the degree to which diversity, equity, and inclusion programs are mainstreamed in this force. These issues upset many people. They upset people on the right who believe such programs have no place in a department dedicated to national defense. They have a central place among those who believe the department needs to represent the great diversity of this country. This debate plays out in our daily public discourse, and it's reflected in this document, too. A lot of that red-meat populism comes through. But as a statement of defense policy, this is the center-of-mass of what we had from 2017 to 2021—some of it good, some of it really good, some of it less good.

The first thing we'll discuss is on page 91, the first page of Chapter 4. It says: "The DoD is also a deeply troubled institution. Historically, the military has been one of America's most trusted institutions, but years of sustained misuse, a two-tier culture of accountability that shields senior officers and officials while exposing junior officers and soldiers in the field, wasteful spending, wildly shifting security policies, exceedingly poor discipline in program execution, and most recently, the Biden administration's profoundly unserious equity agenda and vaccine mandates have taken a serious toll."

There is widespread agreement that senior officers are shielded from accountability. It is evident that there has been insufficient accountability, particularly in acquisition, for decision-makers on programs with unsuccessful outcomes. However, the assertion that junior officers and soldiers are disproportionately exposed is a populist oversimplification. These personnel are, in fact, better cared for, led, supplied, and trained than at any point in military history; the claim to the contrary is hyperbolic.

The vaccine mandate is another example of populist rhetoric. The recommendation to reinstate personnel to duty with back pay is problematic. While it is conceivable that these individuals were following lawful orders at the time, a policy mitigating the consequences of what is now considered a flawed decision could be implemented. However, widespread agreement with the vaccine mandate issue is contingent upon the reinstatement of those discharged for homosexuality. Given that these individuals willfully disobeyed lawful orders, the consequences were justified.

The sentiment associated with admirals and generals getting away with things while lower-level officers and enlisted are punished is primarily due to two things during the first Trump administration and early Biden administration. One is the Navy SEAL, who was accused of a war crime and all the controversy around that. Remember, we lost a Secretary of the Navy over that, who tried to work around the President with the SECNAV or the administration and the Chief of Staff to reach some agreement that would be win-win in his mind. That didn't play well with Secretary Esper. The other sentiment is about the American service members lost at Abbey Gate during the exit from Afghanistan, particularly the pullout from Kabul, and how nobody lost their jobs over that, especially General McKenzie. I think that sentiment informs this, and we'll discuss those items in more detail as we go forward.

From page 92 of Project 2025, the next passage we're highlighting states: "Technology is critical to maintaining our warfighting primacy, but we must be wary of the siren song that technology alone can protect us." This is a reasonable statement. Examining the current Pentagon leadership reveals individuals who appear more suited to Silicon Valley or SpaceX roles. These individuals are preoccupied with technology, believing it can eliminate mass and capacity, which is occasionally accurate. However, this reliance on technology may have reached excessive levels. Regarding the Navy force structure, assertions that unmanned systems will render manned platforms obsolete are exaggerated. Describing technology as a "siren song" is a valuable corrective.

A few paragraphs down, it says: "Military service is the most difficult task we ask of our citizens, and our nation is enormously blessed that so many young patriotic Americans eagerly volunteer to carry such a heavy burden. We owe them everything, and we must do better. To do better, however, means recognizing and implementing four overriding priorities: Priority number one, reestablish a culture of command accountability, non-politicization, and warfighting focus. Priority number two is to transform our armed forces for maximum effectiveness in an era of great power competition. Priority three is to provide necessary support to Department of Homeland Security border protection operations. Border protection is a national security issue that requires sustained attention and effort by all elements of the executive branch. Priority number four, demand financial transparency and accountability."

There are no objectionable elements in any of them.

The next sub-chapter is "DoD Policy," which states: "By far the most significant danger to American security, freedoms, and prosperity is China. China is, by any measure, the most powerful state in the world other than the United States itself. It apparently aspires to dominate Asia and then, from that position, become globally preeminent. If Beijing could achieve this goal, it could dramatically undermine America's core interests, including by restricting U.S. access to the world's most important market. Preventing this from happening must be the top priority for American foreign and defense policy. Accordingly, the United States must ensure that China does not succeed. This requires a denial defense—the ability to make the subordination of Taiwan or other U.S. allies in Asia prohibitively difficult. Critically, the United States must be able to do this at a level of cost and risk that Americans are willing to bear, given the relative importance of Taiwan to China and to the U.S."

This passage contains some interesting intellectual discussion. Specifically, it mentions "denial defense." This gets back to deterrence theory, specifically conventional deterrence theory. Do you deter someone more effectively by being over the horizon with lots of weapons and saying, "If you do that, we will punish you," which is deterrence by punishment? You hope the other guy refrains from aggression out of fear of punishment, even though the chances of initial success in his aggression are higher. Or do you deter by denial, which states that we're going to be there, powerful, networked, and lethal, making the first move unappealing because it will likely be denied, or the timetable for success will be extended unreasonably? There are big-picture thoughts here. One perspective advocates for a deterrence-by-denial strategy. This viewpoint was supported in the 2017 National Security Strategy and the 2018 National Defense Strategy. It is considered an effective means of deterring China. In contrast, the current Biden administration leans towards deterrence by punishment. Both approaches have historical precedent and are considered reasonable; however, there is disagreement with the current administration's chosen approach.

The next passage reiterates initial impressions. It says: "The United States and its allies also face real threats from Russia, as evidenced by Vladimir Putin's brutal war in Ukraine." This statement might surprise those who follow either progressive or conservative television news, given its source from a conservative think tank. It continues: "As well as from Iran, North Korea, and transnational terrorism. At a time when decades of ill-advised military operations in the Greater Middle East, the atrophy of the defense industrial base, and the impact of sequestration—that effort to balance the budget during the Obama administration seriously kneecapped the defense budget for years afterward, which was an unintended consequence of a poison pill that folks never thought they would take—and effective disarmament by many U.S. allies have exacted a high toll on America's military. This is a grim landscape. The United States needs to deal with these threats forthrightly and with strength, but it also needs to be realistic. It cannot wish away these problems; rather, it must confront them with a clear-eyed recognition of the need for choice, discipline, and adequate resources for defense. In this light, U.S. defense strategy must identify China unequivocally as the top priority for U.S. defense planning while modernizing and expanding the U.S. nuclear arsenal and sustaining an efficient and effective counterterrorism enterprise. U.S. allies must also step up, with some joining the United States in taking on China in Asia, while others must take more of a lead in dealing with threats from Russia in Europe, Iran in the Middle East, and North Korea."

These points require more discussion later, as the document specifies responsibilities for facing Russia or China.

The reality is that achieving these goals will require more spending on defense by the United States and its allies, active support for reindustrialization, and increased support for allies' productive capacity to scale our efforts together.

The words and concepts are not controversial. But it's notable when you contextualize them and recognize that this document is from the Heritage Foundation, which has been hostile to American support for Ukraine. They discuss Putin's brutal war in Ukraine while simultaneously suggesting that Europeans need to spend more on defense, sowing the seeds for poking at NATO and even advocating for leaving NATO. This document contains seeds of extremism. It's not an extremist statement, but extremists could interpret it as supporting their views. They say there's a brutal war in Ukraine but then imply it's not Europe's problem. They also say we need Europe to help us with China, which is inconsistent if we criticize rich European nations for insufficient defense spending but not Australia, Thailand, Taiwan, South Korea, and Japan. Theoretically, we are inconsistent. We're all in on China, as stated in this document and by the first Trump administration. This inconsistency is troubling. They criticize European allies for not spending enough on defense but excuse Asian allies for the same behavior.

The next passage, in Chapter 4, states: "This focus and priority for U.S. defense activities will deny China the first island chain." The statement identifies the denying of China access beyond the first island chain. Subparagraphs to that statement are:

- All U.S. defense efforts, from force planning to employment and posture, must focus on ensuring the ability of American forces to prevail in the pacing scenario and deny China a fait accompli against Taiwan.

- Prioritizing the U.S. conventional force planning construct to defeat a Chinese invasion of Taiwan before allocating resources to other missions, such as simultaneously fighting another conflict.

Denying China a fait accompli against Taiwan is crucial. However, there's an internal inconsistency in advocating for 50,000 more people in the Army and a larger Air Force to handle two major regional contingencies (2MRCs). Either we want to be a 2MRC Department of Defense, or we're all in on China.

In subparagraph 3 of this bullet, labeled "Increase Allied Conventional Defense Burden Sharing," it states: "Transform NATO so that U.S. allies can field the majority of the conventional forces required to deter Russia while relying on the United States primarily for our nuclear deterrent and select other capabilities, while reducing the U.S. force posture in Europe." This is groundbreaking and troubling. The majority of the conventional forces required to deter Russia are already fielded by NATO allies, not the United States. Relying on the United States primarily for nuclear deterrence means we're not a European conventional arms strategy player. This could lead to either a drastic change in NATO or the beginning of its end, as Europeans might seek to secure their own defense without the U.S. This stance could force European allies, which might not benefit American national security.

American national security should be executed autonomously, free from influence by the domestic political considerations of other nations. The United States should possess the capability to act independently or in conjunction with allies. This perspective underpins certain strategies, but coercing European allies could potentially undermine American security.

The term "transform NATO" is open to interpretation and could be construed as synonymous with "dismantle NATO," as NATO without significant United States leadership is not NATO. The previous administration emphasized the concept of European nations contributing their fair share to NATO, which appears reasonable on its face. However, this perspective has been contextualized by suggesting that the United States has historically contributed a fair share relative to its GDP and defense budget. As discussions evolve around Europe assuming a more prominent leadership role and developing defense strategies independent of the United

States, a shift in attitude is becoming evident. Consequently, the phrase "transform NATO" might accurately reflect a desire to dismantle the alliance.

In WESTPAC, paragraph 5, or subparagraph 5, says: "Enable South Korea to take the lead in its conventional defense against North Korea." The million-man South Korean army indicates this is already happening. The suggestion that South Korea does not take the lead in its defense is just wrong.

An in-depth analysis of the nuclear triad is beyond the scope of this discussion. However, before transitioning to the topic of acquisition, it is necessary to review the provided information. "Expand and modernize the U.S. nuclear force so that it has the size, sophistication, and tailoring to deter China and Russia simultaneously." This appears to involve two primary objectives:

- Develop a new nuclear arsenal with increased size, sophistication, and tailored capabilities, including new theater-level options.
- Ensure that the United States possesses a nuclear arsenal sufficient to deter any potential nuclear coercion.

On DoD acquisition and sustainment, it talks about allowing the acquisition community to focus on portfolio management and move money around more efficiently instead of being locked into inflexible multi-year procurement cycles. It is desirable to grant the Director of Surface Warfare authority to reallocate funds from lower to higher priority areas within a portfolio during the execution year. However, Congress is highly protective of such authorities. While existing pilot programs address portfolio management, their effectiveness and outcomes should be evaluated before implementing this as a broader defense policy.

Both protective instincts and the creation of winners and losers influence congressional oversight. Based on emerging tactical needs, unilateral decisions by the Director of Air Warfare or Surface Warfare can impact constituencies. For example, shifting contracts between companies can affect job markets in different regions. Such decisions, made in the interest of national defense, could have negative electoral consequences for lawmakers.

The notion that removing appropriations and authorization processes would improve spending efficiency is overly simplistic. These processes are integral to the system and cannot be easily bypassed. Pilot programs that grant services limited flexibility in fund allocation are commendable, but significantly reducing congressional spending involvement is unrealistic.

The defense acquisition process is complex and influenced by various factors. Lawmakers often prioritize funding for programs within their districts, even if they advocate for overall budget cuts. This behavior contributes to increased defense spending as it necessitates a system of incentives to maintain political support. The Base Realignment and Closure (BRAC) process exemplifies how local interests can hinder cost-saving measures and undermine national defense objectives. These factors underscore the complexity of the defense budget process.

## Controversial DoD Personnel Reforms and Recruitment Strategies

Then we get into DoD personnel, which is the most left-right binary part of the document. It discusses the reforms that are needed: rescue recruiting and retention.

- Subparagraph one: appoint a special assistant to the president to liaise with Congress, DoD, and other interested parties on recruiting and retention.
- Two: improve recruiting by suspending the use of the recently introduced MHS Genesis system, which uses private medical records of potential recruits at military entrance processing stations (MEPS), creating unnecessary delays and unwanted rejections.
- Three: improve military recruiters' access to secondary schools and require completion of the Armed Services Vocational Aptitude Battery (ASVAB).

A special assistant to the president for recruiting could be useful. Using private health records has slowed things down and kept potential recruits out. Requiring the ASVAB for high school students might expose more people to the military, but it could also lead to people not taking it seriously.

The demand is twofold: hit your recruiting numbers and make everyone take the ASVAB. This might make it harder for recruiters to hit their numbers. Some suggest that the military's job is to get individuals with baseline qualifications, including physical fitness, and then shape them once they are in the door. So, requiring an aptitude test might deter potential recruits.

It says, "Restore standards of lethality and excellence. Entrance criteria for military service and specific career fields should be based on the needs of those positions. Exceptions for individuals predisposed to require medical treatment—for example, HIV-positive or suffering from gender dysphoria—should be removed, and those with gender dysphoria should be expelled from military service. Physical fitness requirements should be based on the occupational field without consideration of gender, race, ethnicity, or orientation." The topic is emotionally charged and divisive due to its alignment with polarizing aspects of American society. While it is acknowledged that incorporating individuals requiring extensive ongoing medical care into the military could pose financial challenges, it is debatable whether this responsibility should fall to the armed forces. This represents a policy stance of the current administration and aligns with their electoral strategy. A potential issue arises when this preference becomes a campaign pledge or a prerequisite for service. For example, a prospective Secretary of Defense might be compelled to agree with excluding individuals with gender dysphoria from military service to secure their position.

The following paragraphs fall under the charge that the military is "woke." It says, "Eliminate politicization, reestablish trust and accountability, and restore faith in the force." In 2021, the Reagan National Defense Survey found that only 45% of Americans have "a great deal of trust and confidence in the military," down from 70% in 2018. To build on the gender dysphoria and HIV-positive mandate, it says to instruct senior Military Officers to ensure their primary duty is the Readiness of the Armed Forces, not pursuing a social engineering agenda. This should be reinforced during the Senate confirmation process. Orders and direction motivated by partisan motives should be identified as threats to Readiness.

What about homosexuals? It also says to "eliminate Marxist indoctrination and critical race theory programs and abolish diversity, equity, and inclusion offices. Restrict the use of social media solely for recruitment and discipline any armed services personnel who use an official command channel to engage with civilian critics on social media. This is very specific. Audit course offerings at military academies to remove Marxist indoctrination, eliminate tenure for academic professionals, and apply the same rules to instructors as other DoD contracting personnel. Finally, reverse policies allowing transgender individuals to serve in the military. Gender dysphoria is deemed incompatible with military service, and public monies should not be used for transgender surgeries or to facilitate abortion for service members."

There is general agreement with certain points presented. The characterization of individuals as inherently inferior, weak, or Marxist based on their beliefs is considered inappropriate. The system of government is designed to facilitate disagreement and compromise. However, contemporary political discourse and legislative practices prioritize ideological purity over negotiation. This document reflects this trend.

While there is no theoretical opposition to the concepts presented and the elimination of factors hindering military readiness, using terms such as "Marxism" and "social engineering" warrants specific examples. Concrete instances of programs, lectures, or high-ranking officials prioritizing social engineering are necessary to substantiate these claims. Broad generalizations do not accurately reflect the current state of the military. Recent observations aboard the USS

Harry S. Truman demonstrate a motivated, competent, and mission-focused crew representing diverse backgrounds.

While dividing Americans into identity groups is undesirable, this practice has been prevalent since the nation's founding. The United States is characterized by its diversity, with individuals retaining unique identities. The challenge arises when attributing specific talents to particular identity groups. Evaluations should prioritize individual merit over group affiliation.

The beauty of the military is that job performance and mission accomplishment are self-evident. When higher-ups force identity-based policies, it creates unnecessary divisions. A good unit advances people based on performance, not identity. Issues arise when individuals are promoted based on identity over mission performance.

There's a paragraph called "Reduce the number of generals." It says, "Rank creep is pervasive. The number of O-6 to O-9 officers is at an all-time high across the armed services, above World War II levels, and the actual battlefield experience of this officer corps is at an all-time low. The next president should limit the continued advancement of many of the existing cadres, many of whom have been advanced by prior administrations for reasons other than their war-fighting prowess." This is another "show your work" statement. Review the annual Proceedings magazine lists every flag and general officer by billet. Identify who needs to go, why, and how you will compensate for their loss. This broad brush criticism lacks specificity.

The assertion that senior military officers are unnecessary is a populist oversimplification. These officers hold positions requiring Senate confirmation and possess significant responsibilities. Eliminating this rank structure would be detrimental.

This criticism aligns with the rhetoric employed by Senator Tuberville, who is currently obstructing officer promotions. Such actions unfairly impede the career progression of numerous dedicated service members. Those should be addressed if specific instances of wasteful or redundant positions can be identified. However, a blanket condemnation of the officer corps lacks specificity.

## Evaluating Service-Specific Initiatives in Project 2025

Starting with the Army, subparagraph 4 under "Rebuild the Army" says, "Increase the Army force structure by 50,000 to handle two major regional contingencies simultaneously." This goes back to trying to have it both ways: focusing on China while maintaining an army big enough to fight two wars at once.

It's internally inconsistent, and they should be called to account for it. It also says, "Focus on deployability and sustained operations. The U.S. Army's very lethal ground force capability is irrelevant if it cannot quickly deploy to locations for employment and decisive operations to secure our global security interests. Additionally, if Army logisticians provide ground transportation, fuel, food and water, munitions, medical supplies and services, and veterinary services that are critical to the sustainment of the other services, deployability of the Army is an issue. Sea lift is an issue. Sea lift ships are place where we could begin to build immediately. We could get hot production lines and increase our number of ships. The Army doesn't want to pay for it, and so we wind up with less ability to close the force than we need."

Another element of the culture war under the Army section is "Transform Army culture and training. The Army can no longer serve as the nation's social testing ground. A rebuilt Army focused again on its core warfighting mission and empowered with the tools, resources, and authorities it needs to accomplish that mission must be the next administration's highest defense priority." Subparagraph 1: "Stop using the Army as a testbed for social evolution. Misusing the Army in this way detracts from its core purpose while doing little to reshape the American social structure." They call this a lose-lose. "The Army no longer reflects national demographics to the degree it did before 1974 when the draft was eliminated." Paragraph 2: "Demand accountability in senior leaders to reverse the decline in public support for military service." A rebuilt Army focused on its core warfighting mission and empowered with the tools, resources, and authorities it needs to accomplish that mission must be the next administration's highest defense priority. That's the number one priority, according to this document.

But why? When you say that's the highest priority, it just becomes rhetoric. "Demand accountability for senior leaders to reverse the decline in public support for military service." One reason for the decline is that many more financially rewarding options exist for young people. While money can't solve everything, increasing pay for junior enlisted personnel could attract more recruits. Instead of blaming senior leaders, consider the broader economic and social factors.

No, it's not right. One political party doesn't see military service as part of its values, while the other side tells its dependents that the military is bad. No wonder recruiting is difficult.

As we look at each service's sections, it's clear that the Army, Navy, Air Force, Marine, and Space Force reps didn't communicate. There was no continuity control in the editing process. You can tell where each author stands politically, especially regarding social experimentation.

In the Navy section, there's no mention of culture or social engineering. It says, "Invest in and expand force structure. The Navy's organizing principle remains platform-centered vessels manned by sailors." However, there's no granularity. The document states, "Build a fleet of more than 355 ships," but doesn't specify the types of ships. The Marines mention the amphibs disparity, but the Navy section lacks detail on aircraft carriers, destroyers, frigates, or submarines. This Navy section is not well-written or developed. It has a few big ideas, like maintaining platform-centered vessels manned by sailors and developing unmanned systems to augment the manned force. Unmanned in support of manned is the right approach to fleet design and force structure.

The absence of social engineering themes in the document is unexpected. However, the document's committee-based authorship and apparent lack of thorough editing may account for this omission. While there is a lack of specific ship numbers and types, the document's focus on high-level defense strategy justifies this omission. Given the expertise within the relevant communities, more detailed force structure assessments are expected to follow. The goal of a 355-ship fleet is essentially a call for increased naval funding, as achieving and maintaining such a force would require an additional $40 billion annually.

Then there's a paragraph about the general board, which seems a little incongruous with the theme of each service.

"Reestablish the general board. In contrast with the Navy general board that served ship development well during the interwar period, the current joint process for defining the requirements for major defense acquisitions is not well suited to long-term planning needed for USN fleet architecture and shipbuilding. The interwar general board should serve as a model, empowered with final decision authority over all requirements documents concerning ships and the major defense systems fielded on ships. The individual board members would ensure a broad base of knowledge as well as independent thinking."

The proposed concept appears to overlap with existing OPNAV staff responsibilities, specifically those of the warfare directors. The rationale for this proposal remains unclear. There is a prevailing sentiment among naval professionals that shipbuilding requirements and acquisition processes should be managed independently of the joint process. Including the Flight III Arleigh Burke destroyer and FFG(X) programs within the JROC process is cited as evidence of this issue. While the argument for a dedicated shipbuilding process is valid, the proposed reestablishment of the General Board does not fully capture the extent to which DoD-level and joint staff procedures impede shipbuilding.

Then, it talks about accelerating the purchase of key munitions. "It takes years to build and maintain navies but only hours to expend their ordnance in combat. The Navy must be prepared to expend large quantities of air-launched and sea-launched stealthy precision cruise missiles against both targets at sea and ashore. Additionally, modern air defense requires the use of high-performance surface-to-air missiles." This lesson is learned from recent Houthi experiences in the Red Sea. It discusses producing key munitions at maximum capacity and working with Congress to enhance the munition supply chains and workforce.

What's missing here is directed energy. Whether we're talking Air Force, Navy, Army, or Marines, we may fight an industrial power that can outproduce us missile for missile. Continuing to match them missile for missile is futile. We need other capabilities, like directed energy: lasers, high-powered microwaves. There's none of that here. The Navy needs a moonshot to develop and test a high-powered laser at sea within the next three years. Money needs to go towards this. We need to tell the acquisition community that this is valued.

That should be a huge foot-stomper in this section. Then it talks about enhancing warfighter development. While discussing reducing the number of general and flag officers, it says, "Elevate the headquarters staff focused on warfighter development (N7) within the office of the Chief of Naval Operations and empower it to develop such requirements." Interestingly, this section is generalized yet specific about empowering N7 in the Pentagon.

The Air Force section identifies specific platforms. The Air Force is generally better at acquisition than the Navy. Needed reforms: increase spending and budget accuracy in line with a threat-based strategy. Subparagraph 1: "Adopt a two-war force defense strategy." This contradicts the earlier high-level tenets with scenarios for each service, allowing the Air Force to attain resources by developing a force-sizing construct reflecting strategic objectives. "Increase the Air Force budget by 5% annually after adjusting for inflation to reverse the decline in size, age, and readiness and facilitate the transition to a more modern, lethal, and survivable force."

They put an exact number on it and specify how to use the money. "Increase F-35 procurement to 60-80 per year. Build the B-21 at 15-18 aircraft per year. Increase airlift refueling capacity to support agile combat employment. Develop and buy a larger quantity of advanced mid-range weapons (50-200 nautical miles) and size to maximize targets per sortie for stealth aircraft flying in contested environments against target sets that could exceed 100,000 aim points." These are specific requirements, which is great.

They also talk about accelerating the production of the Sentinel ICBM to reduce reliance on the Minuteman III. "Increase the number of EC-37 Bravo electronic warfare aircraft from 10 to 20," a China-facing requirement. They invest in the future of the Air Force, discussing cyber and electromagnetic spectrum capabilities. The Air Force section has a more actionable framework than the Navy's.

## Missile Defense and the China Focus

There is a nuclear deterrent section, but it is notable that throughout the discussion, the primary focus has been on China. Missile defense is not addressed until the final portion of the document. The term "hypersonic" appears only once, on page 125, within the Department of Defense chapter. One would expect each service, particularly the Navy responsible for defending the fleet in the Western Pacific, to have extensively addressed missile deterrence and its corresponding capabilities.

The new missile spotted under the wing of Super Hornets, the AARGM-ER, is basically an SM-6 mounted on a fighter that, on paper, should be able to out-stick the PL-17 that their J-16s carry. That is the carrier killer weapon because critics of carrier air power say it's vulnerable. If you're talking about the PL, the aircraft carrier is the first thing to go, and it's an easy target because you don't have anything that can reach out and touch the Chinese fighters before they can commit weapons against you. Again, in this document, it seems like missile defense is somewhat of an afterthought.

# 11. Implementation Strategies

## Major Plans and Programs

Implementing Project 2025 requires a series of well-coordinated plans and programs across various governance domains. These plans and programs are designed to ensure that the next conservative administration can effectively govern from day one, achieve its policy objectives, and address the nation's key challenges. Below is a detailed overview of the major plans and programs under Project 2025.

### ***Policy Development and Refinement***

- <u>Comprehensive Policy Guide</u>: Develop a detailed policy guide that outlines specific recommendations for each federal agency and department. This guide will be the blueprint for the administration's actions and decisions.
- <u>Continuous Research</u>: Conduct ongoing research and analysis to refine and update policy proposals based on emerging data, trends, and stakeholder feedback.

- <u>Expert Collaboration</u>: Collaborate with experts from various fields to ensure that policy recommendations are well-informed, practical, and aligned with conservative principles.

## ***Personnel Recruitment and Training***

- <u>Personnel Database</u>: Maintain a comprehensive database of qualified individuals who align with the conservative agenda and are prepared to fill critical administrative roles.

- <u>Vetting and Selection</u>: Implement a rigorous vetting process to ensure all candidates meet the required qualifications and adhere to the administration's values and principles.

- <u>Presidential Administration Academy</u>: Establish the Presidential Administration Academy to provide training and education for incoming officials. The academy will offer online courses and in-person seminars covering government operations, policy implementation, and leadership skills.

## ***Transition Planning and Execution***

- <u>Detailed Transition Plans</u>: Develop detailed transition plans for each federal agency and department, outlining key actions and priorities for the first 100 days and beyond.

- <u>Transition Teams</u>: Form transition teams to oversee the handover of responsibilities, ensure continuity, and address any immediate challenges.

- <u>Executive Orders</u>: Prepare a series of executive orders to be issued on day one, setting the administration's tone and signaling its policy priorities.

## ***Regulatory Reform and Government Efficiency***

- <u>Regulatory Review</u>: Conduct a comprehensive review of existing regulations to identify outdated, unnecessary, or overly burdensome ones. Develop a plan to repeal or reform these regulations.

- <u>Streamlining Operations</u>: Implement measures to streamline government operations, reduce redundancies, and improve efficiency. This includes consolidating functions and departments where appropriate.

- <u>Accountability Measures</u>: Introduce accountability measures to ensure federal agencies and cmployees are held responsible for their performance and adherence to the administration's goals.

## ***Economic and Tax Policy***

- <u>Tax Reform</u>: Implement comprehensive tax reform to simplify the tax code, lower tax rates, and eliminate loopholes. The goal is to create a fairer and more efficient tax system that promotes economic growth.

- <u>Deregulation</u>: Reduce government interference in the economy by eliminating unnecessary regulations and promoting free market policies.

- <u>Fiscal Responsibility</u>: Develop a plan to reduce government spending, balance the federal budget, and address the national debt. This includes identifying areas where cuts can be made without compromising essential services.

## ***National Security and Defense***

- <u>Strengthening the Military</u>: Ensure the United States maintains a robust and capable military to defend against external threats. This includes investing in new technologies, modernizing equipment, and improving training programs.

- <u>Border Security</u>: Implement policies to strengthen border security and enforce immigration laws. This includes building physical barriers, increasing the number of border patrol agents, and utilizing advanced surveillance technologies.

- <u>Foreign Policy</u>: Pursue a foreign policy that prioritizes American interests and values, promoting peace and stability through strength. This includes strengthening alliances, countering adversaries, and promoting free trade.

## ***Social and Domestic Policies***

- <u>Family-Centric Policies</u>: Implement policies that strengthen families, promote marriage, and support parents in their role as primary educators and caregivers. This includes eliminating marriage penalties and reinstating work requirements for welfare programs.

- <u>Healthcare Reform</u>: Develop and implement a comprehensive healthcare reform plan that increases access, reduces costs, and improves the quality of care. This includes promoting competition, increasing transparency, and expanding health savings accounts.

- <u>Education Reform</u>: Promote policies that expand school choice options for parents and students, ensuring access to quality education regardless of socioeconomic status. This includes supporting charter schools, voucher programs, and homeschooling.

## ***Environmental and Energy Policies***

- <u>Practical Environmentalism</u>: Promote environmental policies that balance conservation with economic growth, emphasizing innovation and private sector solutions. This includes reducing regulatory burdens and promoting sustainable practices.

- <u>Energy Independence</u>: Support policies that enhance American energy independence by developing domestic energy resources and reducing regulatory barriers. This includes promoting the use of renewable energy sources and advancing technological innovations.

## ***Civic Responsibility and National Unity***

- <u>Civic Education</u>: Promote civic education that instills an understanding of American history, values, and constitutional principles. This includes supporting programs that educate citizens about their rights and responsibilities.

- <u>National Service</u>: Encourage voluntary national service programs that foster a sense of civic duty and national unity. This includes supporting initiatives that provide opportunities for young people to serve their communities and country.

- <u>Community Engagement</u>: Support initiatives that strengthen local communities and encourage citizen involvement in addressing local issues. This includes promoting volunteerism and supporting community-based organizations.

## ***Continuous Monitoring and Evaluation***

- <u>Performance Metrics</u>: Develop and implement performance metrics to track the progress and impact of policies and programs. This includes regularly reviewing and assessing the effectiveness of implemented measures.

- <u>Stakeholder Feedback</u>: Solicit feedback from stakeholders, including policymakers, experts, and the public, to ensure that the administration's actions are aligned with its goals and values.

- <u>Adaptation and Improvement</u>: Use data and feedback to refine and improve policies and programs continuously. This includes making necessary adjustments to address emerging challenges and opportunities.

## **Funding and Resource Allocation**

Effective implementation of Project 2025 requires careful planning and allocation of financial and human resources. Securing adequate funding and ensuring efficient use of resources are crucial for achieving the project's goals. Below is a detailed overview of the funding and resource allocation strategies within Project 2025.

### ***Securing Funding***

<u>Private Donations and Grants:</u>

- Conservative Foundations: Engage with conservative foundations and philanthropic organizations that align with the goals of Project 2025. These entities can provide substantial financial support through grants and donations.

- Individual Donors: Launch fundraising campaigns targeting donors committed to conservative principles. Utilize digital platforms, events, and direct mail to reach potential supporters.

<u>Corporate Sponsorships:</u>

- Aligned Corporations: Partner with corporations that share the project's values and objectives. These partnerships can provide financial contributions, in-kind support, and other resources.

- Sponsorship Programs: Develop sponsorship programs that offer recognition and benefits to corporate sponsors, encouraging long-term support.

<u>Crowdfunding:</u>

- Online Campaigns: Utilize crowdfunding platforms to reach a broader audience. Create compelling campaigns highlighting the importance and impact of

Project 2025, encouraging small donations from many supporters.

## **_Budget Planning and Management_**

Comprehensive Budgeting:

- Initial Budget Plan: Develop a detailed budget plan that outlines the estimated costs for each phase of Project 2025, including policy development, personnel recruitment, training, transition planning, and implementation.
- Regular Updates: Continuously update the budget plan based on actual expenditures and changing needs. Ensure all budget adjustments align with the project's goals and priorities.

Financial Oversight:

- Transparency: Maintain transparency in all financial dealings by regularly publishing financial reports and updates. This builds trust with donors and stakeholders.
- Accountability: Establish a financial oversight committee to monitor expenditures and ensure funds are used effectively and responsibly.

## **_Resource Allocation_**

Personnel Resources:

- Recruitment Strategy: Implement a strategic recruitment plan to attract qualified, committed individuals. Focus on building a diverse team with expertise in various policy areas.

- Training Programs: Allocate resources to the Presidential Administration Academy to ensure that all incoming personnel receive comprehensive training on government operations, policy implementation, and leadership skills.

Technology and Infrastructure:

- IT Systems: Invest in robust IT systems and infrastructure to support the project's operations. This includes secure databases, communication platforms, and data analytics tools.

- Office Space: Secure appropriate office space for the project team and transition staff. Ensure that the facilities are equipped with the necessary resources and technology.

## ***Leveraging Partnerships and Collaborations***

Inter-Organizational Collaboration:

- Conservative Organizations: Collaborate with other conservative organizations to share resources, expertise, and best practices. This enhances the project's capacity and effectiveness.

- Think Tanks and Research Institutions: Partner with think tanks and institutions to access cutting-edge research, data, and policy analysis.

<u>Government and Public Sector:</u>

- Public-Private Partnerships: Develop public-private partnerships to leverage additional resources and expertise. This can include collaborations with local and state governments, educational institutions, and non-profit organizations.

- Federal Grants and Programs: Identify and apply for federal grants and programs that align with the goals of Project 2025. These funds can support specific initiatives and projects within the broader framework.

## ***Resource Optimization and Efficiency***

<u>Cost-Effective Solutions:</u>

- Operational Efficiency: Implement cost-effective solutions for project operations, such as utilizing digital tools for communication and collaboration, minimizing travel expenses, and optimizing office space usage.

- Procurement Policies: Establish efficient procurement policies to ensure that goods and services are purchased at competitive prices without compromising quality.

Performance Monitoring:

- Key Performance Indicators (KPIs): Develop KPIs to monitor the performance and impact of various initiatives and programs. Use these metrics to allocate resources more effectively and make data-driven decisions.

- Regular Reviews: Conduct regular reviews and evaluations of resource allocation to identify areas for improvement and ensure that resources are being used optimally.

## ***Sustainability and Long-Term Planning***

Long-Term Funding Strategies:

- Endowment Fund: Establish an endowment fund to provide a sustainable funding source for Project 2025. Encourage major donors to contribute to this fund to ensure the project's financial stability.

- Legacy Giving: Promote legacy giving options, such as bequests and charitable trusts, to secure long-term financial support from committed supporters.

Future Planning:

- Scalability: Plan for the scalability of Project 2025 by identifying potential future needs and opportunities for expansion. Ensure that the project can adapt to changing circumstances and continue to achieve its goals.

- Continuous Improvement: Foster a culture of continuous improvement by regularly assessing the project's performance and making necessary adjustments to strategies and resource allocation.

By securing adequate funding and efficiently allocating resources, Project 2025 can ensure the successful implementation of its plans and programs. These strategies provide a clear framework for financial and resource management, enabling the project to achieve its goals and make a lasting impact on American governance.

## Presidential Transition Plans

The Presidential Transition Plans are critical to ensuring a smooth and effective power transfer to the incoming conservative administration. These plans provide detailed guidelines and actions to be taken before, during, and after the transition, ensuring continuity, stability, and the swift implementation of the administration's policy agenda. Below is a detailed overview of the Presidential Transition Plans under Project 2025.

### *Pre-Election Phase (2024 Q1 - Q3)*

Early Planning and Coordination:

- Establish Transition Team: Form a dedicated transition team comprising experienced policymakers, legal experts, and administrative professionals. This team will be responsible for overseeing all aspects of the transition process.
- Engage Stakeholders: Engage key stakeholders, including current government officials, conservative organizations, and potential appointees, to gather insights and build support for the transition.

Develop Transition Framework:

- Policy Review: Conduct a comprehensive review of existing policies and identify areas that require immediate attention or reform. Develop a policy framework that aligns with the administration's goals.
- Draft Transition Plans: Create detailed transition plans for each federal agency and department, outlining key actions, priorities, and timelines for the first 100 days and beyond.

Training and Preparation:

- Presidential Administration Academy: Launch the Presidential Administration Academy to provide training and education for incoming officials. Focus on government operations, policy implementation, leadership skills, and ethical standards.

- Simulation Exercises: Conduct exercises to prepare the transition team and incoming officials for various scenarios and challenges they may face during the transition.

## ***Election to Inauguration Phase (November 2024 - January 20, 2025)***

<u>Immediate Post-Election Actions:</u>

- Establish Headquarters: Set up a transition headquarters as the central hub for all transition activities. Ensure the headquarters is equipped with the necessary resources and technology.

- Engage with Outgoing Administration: Establish communication channels with the outgoing administration to facilitate a smooth transfer of information, resources, and responsibilities.

<u>Personnel Recruitment and Vetting:</u>

- Finalize Appointments: Finalize the selection of key personnel for cabinet positions, agency heads, and senior advisors. Ensure all appointees are thoroughly vetted and aligned with the administration's values and goals.

- Onboarding and Briefings: Provide comprehensive onboarding and briefings for incoming officials, covering their roles, responsibilities, and the administration's priorities.

<u>Policy Implementation Planning:</u>

- Executive Orders: Prepare a series of executive orders to be issued on day one, addressing immediate policy changes and setting the administration's tone. Ensure that these orders are legally sound and ready for implementation.

- Legislative Agenda: Develop a legislative agenda in collaboration with key congressional leaders, outlining priority bills and initiatives to be introduced in the first 100 days.

## ***Inauguration Day (January 20, 2025)***

<u>Ceremonial and Administrative Actions:</u>

- Inaugural Address: Deliver a clear and inspiring inaugural address that outlines the administration's vision, goals, and commitment to the American people.

- Immediate Executive Actions: Issue the prepared executive orders to initiate immediate policy changes and signal the administration's priorities.

<u>First 24 Hours:</u>

- Staff Meetings: Conduct initial meetings with key cabinet members, agency heads, and senior advisors to establish communication channels and begin coordinating actions.

- Public Communication: Engage with the media and the public to provide updates on the administration's first actions and reassure the nation about the transition process.

## ***First 100 Days (January - April 2025)***

Priority Policy Implementation:

- Focus Areas: Prioritize the implementation of high-impact policies in areas such as tax reform, border security, healthcare, and regulatory reform. Ensure that each agency has clear directives and support for these initiatives.

- Monitoring and Evaluation: Establish mechanisms to monitor and evaluate the progress of policy implementation. Adjust strategies as needed to address challenges and ensure effectiveness.

Legislative Efforts:

- Introduce Key Legislation: Work with Congress to introduce and advance key legislation that aligns with the administration's policy agenda. Build coalitions and negotiate to secure the necessary support for passage.

- Public Advocacy: Utilize public communication and advocacy efforts to build support for the legislative agenda. Engage with stakeholders, interest groups, and the media to promote the administration's initiatives.

Administrative Reforms:

- Regulatory Review: Conduct a thorough review of existing regulations across federal agencies. Identify and eliminate regulations that are outdated, unnecessary, or overly burdensome.
- Efficiency Measures: Implement measures to improve efficiency and effectiveness in government operations. This includes streamlining processes, reducing redundancies, and enhancing accountability.

## ***Long-Term Transition Goals (First Year and Beyond)***

Institutionalizing Reforms:

- Policy Integration: Ensure that key policy reforms are fully integrated into the operations of federal agencies. This involves updating procedures, training staff, and embedding new practices.
- Sustainable Practices: Develop sustainable practices to maintain the effectiveness of implemented policies and reforms. This includes establishing performance metrics and continuous improvement processes.

<u>Building Public Trust:</u>

- Transparency and Accountability: Foster transparency and accountability in all government actions. Regularly communicate with the public and stakeholders about the administration's progress and achievements.
- Engagement and Participation: Encourage public engagement and participation in governance. Create platforms for citizens to provide feedback, raise concerns, and contribute to policy discussions.

<u>Future Planning:</u>

- Leadership Development: Invest in leadership development programs to build a pipeline of future leaders who can continue the administration's work. This includes mentorship, training, and professional development opportunities.
- Long-Term Vision: Develop a long-term vision for the administration's legacy and future goals. Ensure that policies and initiatives are designed to have lasting positive impacts on American society.

By following these detailed Presidential Transition Plans, Project 2025 aims to ensure a seamless transfer of power, effective governance from day one, and the successful implementation of its comprehensive policy agenda.

# 12. The White House and Executive Office

## Structure and Functions

The White House and the Executive Office of the President (EOP) form the nerve center of the federal government, playing a crucial role in implementing the administration's agenda and ensuring efficient governance. Understanding the structure and functions of these entities is essential for effectively navigating the complexities of federal administration and achieving the goals of Project 2025.

### ***The White House Structure:***

<u>The President:</u>

- Role: The President is the chief executive officer of the United States, responsible for enforcing federal laws, directing national policy, and representing the country both domestically and internationally.

- Key Responsibilities: These include signing or vetoing legislation, issuing executive orders, commanding the armed forces, and conducting foreign policy.

<u>The Vice President:</u>

- Role: The Vice President supports the President in their duties and assumes the presidency in the event of the President's incapacity or death.

- Key Responsibilities include presiding over the Senate, casting tie-breaking votes, and representing the administration in various capacities.

## ***White House Offices and Councils:***

<u>Office of the Chief of Staff:</u>

- Function: The Chief of Staff manages White House staff, oversees the implementation of the President's agenda, and serves as the principal advisor to the President.

- Key Units include the Office of Legislative Affairs, Office of Communications, and Office of Management and Administration.

<u>National Security Council (NSC):</u>

- Function: The NSC advises the President on national security and foreign policy matters, coordinating security policy across various agencies.

- Key Units include the Homeland Security Council, the Office of the National Security Advisor, and the National Economic Council.

## Council of Economic Advisers (CEA):

- Function: The CEA provides economic analysis and advice to the President, helping to formulate economic policy.
- Key Units: Includes teams focused on macroeconomic policy, labor markets, and international economics.

## Domestic Policy Council (DPC):

- Function: The DPC advises the President on domestic policy issues, including healthcare, education, and social services.
- Key Units include offices dedicated to health reform, education policy, and welfare programs.

## ***Executive Office of the President (EOP) Structure:***

## Office of Management and Budget (OMB):

- Function: The OMB assists the President in preparing the federal budget, overseeing the implementation of budgetary policies, and managing government finances.
- Key Units: Includes the Budget Review Division, Management and Operations Division, and the Office of Federal Financial Management.

## Office of the United States Trade Representative (USTR):

- Function: The USTR develops and coordinates U.S. international trade policy, negotiates trade agreements, and represents the United States in trade negotiations.

- Key Units: Includes offices focused on trade policy, bilateral and multilateral negotiations, and trade enforcement.

Office of Science and Technology Policy (OSTP):

- Function: The OSTP advises the President on policy decisions' scientific, engineering, and technological aspects and oversees federal research and development programs.

- Key Units: Includes divisions dedicated to science policy, technology innovation, and space policy.

Office of National Drug Control Policy (ONDCP):

- Function: The ONDCP develops and coordinates national drug control policy to reduce illicit drug use and its consequences.

- Key Units include the Office of Public Health and Science, the Office of Criminal Justice, and the Office of State and Local Affairs.

## ***Functions and Responsibilities:***

Policy Development and Coordination:

- Function: The White House and EOP are central to developing and coordinating policy across the federal government. This involves working with Congress, federal agencies, and external stakeholders to formulate and implement the administration's policy agenda.

- Key Activities include drafting policy proposals, preparing legislative initiatives, and coordinating interagency efforts.

<u>Communications and Public Relations:</u>

- Function: The White House manages the administration's communications strategy, ensuring clear and consistent messaging to the public and media.

- Key Activities include conducting press briefings, managing social media accounts, and overseeing public engagement initiatives.

<u>Crisis Management:</u>

- Function: The White House and EOP are responsible for managing national crises, including natural disasters, terrorist attacks, and economic emergencies.

- Key Activities: Includes coordinating federal response efforts, providing public updates, and working with state and local authorities.

Legislative Affairs:

- Function: The White House works closely with Congress to advance the administration's legislative agenda, building support for key initiatives and navigating the legislative process.
- Key Activities: Includes lobbying lawmakers, negotiating with congressional leaders, and monitoring legislative developments.

Administrative Oversight:

- Function: The EOP provides administrative oversight for federal agencies, ensuring they operate efficiently and effectively in line with the administration's goals.
- Key Activities: Includes reviewing agency performance, implementing management reforms, and overseeing regulatory processes.

## ***Key Priorities for Project 2025:***

Streamlining Operations:

- Objective: Improve the efficiency and effectiveness of the White House and EOP operations by streamlining processes, reducing redundancies, and enhancing coordination among various offices.
- Actions: Implement modern management practices, invest in technology upgrades, and promote a culture of continuous improvement.

## Enhancing Transparency and Accountability:

- Objective: To build public trust and ensure ethical governance by fostering transparency and accountability in all White House and EOP activities.
- Actions: Establish clear reporting mechanisms, conduct regular audits, and promote open communication with the public and media.

## Strengthening Policy Development:

- Objective: Enhance the quality and impact of policy development by leveraging expert insights, data-driven analysis, and stakeholder engagement.
- Actions: Expand collaboration with think tanks and research institutions, increase investment in data analytics, and promote interdisciplinary policy development teams.

## Improving Crisis Response:

- Objective: Bolster the administration's ability to respond effectively to national crises by improving planning, coordination, and communication.
- Actions: Develop comprehensive crisis response plans, conduct regular drills and simulations, and enhance coordination with state and local authorities.

# Key Personnel and Roles

The White House and Executive Office of the President (EOP) encompass many key personnel who play crucial roles in implementing the administration's agenda and ensuring effective governance. Understanding the responsibilities and functions of these key personnel is essential for the smooth operation of the executive branch. Below is a detailed overview of the key personnel and their roles within the White House and EOP.

### ***President of the United States:***

- Role: The President is the chief executive officer of the United States, responsible for enforcing federal laws, directing national policy, and representing the country domestically and internationally.

Key Responsibilities:

- Signing or vetoing legislation passed by Congress
- Issuing executive orders to manage operations of the federal government
- Serving as commander-in-chief of the armed forces
- Conducting foreign policy and negotiating treaties
- Appointing federal judges, cabinet members, and other key officials

## ***Vice President of the United States:***

Role: The Vice President supports the President and assumes the presidency in the event of the President's incapacity or death.

Key Responsibilities:

- Presiding over the Senate and casting tie-breaking votes
- Representing the administration at official events and diplomatic engagements
- Advising the President and participating in policy discussions

## ***White House Chief of Staff:***

Role: The Chief of Staff is the highest-ranking employee in the White House, overseeing the Executive Office and serving as the principal advisor to the President.

Key Responsibilities:

- Managing White House staff and operations
- Coordinating policy development and implementation
- Serving as a liaison between the President and other branches of government
- Facilitating communication between the President and key stakeholders

## **National Security Advisor:**

Role: The National Security Advisor advises the President on national security and foreign policy issues, coordinating security policy across various agencies.

Key Responsibilities:

- Leading the National Security Council (NSC)
- Advising the President on national security threats and strategies
- Coordinating interagency efforts on security and foreign policy matters
- Overseeing the implementation of national security policies

## **Director of the Office of Management and Budget (OMB):**

Role: The OMB Director assists the President in preparing the federal budget and overseeing the implementation of budgetary policies.

Key Responsibilities:

- Developing the annual federal budget
- Monitoring government spending and ensuring fiscal responsibility
- Reviewing and approving federal regulations and policies

- Providing policy analysis and advice on budgetary matters

### ***White House Press Secretary:***

Role: The Press Secretary is the primary spokesperson for the President and the administration, managing communications with the media and the public.

Key Responsibilities:

- Conducting daily press briefings
- Managing the administration's media strategy
- Communicating the President's policies and positions to the public
- Responding to media inquiries and managing crisis communications

### ***Senior Advisors and Special Assistants:***

Role: Senior Advisors and Special Assistants provide expertise and counsel to the President on specific policy areas and issues.

Key Responsibilities:

- Advising the President on policy development and implementation
- Coordinating with relevant agencies and stakeholders
- Conducting research and analysis on specific issues

- Assisting in the formulation of strategic initiatives

### *Director of the National Economic Council (NEC):*

Role: The NEC Director advises the President on economic policy and coordinates the administration's economic agenda.

<u>Key Responsibilities:</u>

- Leading the National Economic Council
- Providing economic analysis and policy recommendations
- Coordinating economic policy initiatives across federal agencies
- Advising the President on economic trends and issues

### *Director of the Domestic Policy Council (DPC):*

Role: The DPC Director advises the President on domestic policy issues, including healthcare, education, and social services.

<u>Key Responsibilities:</u>

- Leading the Domestic Policy Council
- Coordinating the development and implementation of domestic policies
- Advising the President on domestic policy trends and issues

- Working with relevant agencies and stakeholders to advance policy initiatives

## **_Director of the Office of National Drug Control Policy (ONDCP):_**

Role: The ONDCP Director develops and coordinates national drug control policy to reduce illicit drug use and its consequences.

Key Responsibilities:

- Leading the Office of National Drug Control Policy
- Coordinating federal efforts to combat drug abuse and trafficking
- Developing strategies to reduce drug demand and supply
- Advising the President on drug control issues and policies

## **_U.S. Trade Representative (USTR):_**

Role: The USTR develops and coordinates U.S. international trade policy, negotiates trade agreements, and represents the United States in trade negotiations.

Key Responsibilities:

- Negotiating and enforcing international trade agreements

- Advising the President on trade policy and issues
- Representing the U.S. in trade disputes and negotiations
- Promoting American economic interests abroad

## *Chief of Staff to the First Lady:*

Role: The Chief of Staff to the First Lady manages the First Lady's office and supports her initiatives and engagements.

Key Responsibilities:

- Overseeing the First Lady's schedule and public appearances
- Coordinating with other White House offices and external stakeholders
- Supporting the First Lady's policy initiatives and programs
- Managing communication and media relations for the First Lady

## *White House Counsel:*

Role: The White House Counsel provides legal advice to the President and the administration on various issues.

Key Responsibilities:

- Advising the President on legal matters and executive orders

- Reviewing legislation and executive actions for legal compliance
- Managing the administration's legal strategy and responses to litigation
- Ensuring adherence to ethical standards and legal protocols

By understanding the roles and responsibilities of these key personnel, Project 2025 aims to ensure that the next conservative administration is equipped with a well-coordinated and effective team. This team will be crucial in implementing the administration's policy agenda, navigating the complexities of federal governance, and addressing the nation's key challenges.

# Conclusion

Project 2025 has sparked significant criticism from various sources. Critics argue that the project embodies a comprehensive plan to centralize executive power, erode democratic norms, and enforce a far-right agenda on American governance and society.

One major criticism is that Project 2025 seeks to expand presidential control over the federal bureaucracy. The plan includes reviving the Schedule F classification, which would allow the president to replace thousands of civil service employees with political appointees loyal to the administration. Critics argue this would undermine the nonpartisan nature of the civil service and politicize federal agencies, making them tools of the executive branch rather than independent entities.

Critics highlight that Project 2025's blueprint includes proposals to dismantle or weaken key democratic institutions. This includes plans to defund the Department of Justice and dismantle the FBI and other agencies that could act as checks on presidential power. Such moves are seen as efforts to undermine the rule of law and enable the executive branch to operate with little oversight or accountability.

Third, the project is criticized for its potential use of government power to target political opponents and critics. There are fears that it would enable the executive to pursue legal action against political adversaries and critical media outlets, drawing parallels to authoritarian regimes where dissent is suppressed through state mechanisms.

The fourth criticism is the social and cultural agenda. Project 2025's policy agenda includes strong positions on social issues, promoting conservative values that critics argue could roll back rights and protections for various groups. The document outlines plans to restrict LGBTQ+ rights, enforce strict anti-abortion measures, and integrate Christian nationalist principles into government policy. This agenda has raised concerns about the erosion of civil liberties and the imposition of a particular religious and ideological framework on the entire nation.

Lastly, there are the environmental and climate policy rollbacks. The project's stance on environmental regulations is contentious. It proposes significant rollbacks of climate policies, which critics argue would have detrimental effects on efforts to combat climate change and protect the environment. This aspect of the plan is seen as catering to business interests at the expense of long-term ecological sustainability.

This ambitious initiative by the Heritage Foundation seeks to reshape numerous facets of American society and governance. From redefining the roles of key federal agencies to proposing sweeping changes in immigration, military policies, and social programs, Project 2025 is positioned to leave a lasting impact.

As citizens and policymakers grapple with the country's future direction, understanding the nuances of such proposals becomes crucial. Project 2025 represents a significant chapter in the ongoing dialogue about America's future, and it is up to all stakeholders to engage thoughtfully and constructively in shaping the path forward.